1.00
11/12

the RED DOOR community

the RED DOOR community

UNDERSTANDING THE ONE SAVIOR OF THE JEWS
AND THE GENTILES, AND HOW THEY WILL EMERGE
TOGETHER TO HONOR HIM

Jeffrey Cranford & Jeff Hopper

LINKS PLAYERS PUBLISHING
A ministry of Links Players International
La Quinta, California

the RED DOOR community

Links Players International is a mission organization committed
to seeing people of influence in the kingdom of the world transformed by Jesus Christ that they may become people of impact
in the kingdom of God. We normally open contact with people
through the game of golf.
Find out more at www.linksplayers.com.

The Red Door Community is also a weekly gathering of men and
women for fellowship and Bible study each week in the Coachella
Valley of California. You are welcome to join us. Find out more at
www.thereddoorcommunity.com.

*To the emerging congregations
of our believing Jewish friends in Israel,
who are boldly following Yeshua
as the Messiah of Promise*

TABLE OF CONTENTS

Introduction A Book of Hope   9

1 The Red Door   15

2 The Red Door Community   21

3 The Gentile Test   25

4 Natural and Wild Together   39

5 A Word about Prophetic Understanding   49

6 Shepherds among the People   55

7 'Pentecost 2'   71

8 Global Impact of Jewish Restoration   89

9 The Role of Gentiles in Ministry to Jews   103

10 The Elisha Ministry
   in Expectancy of the Coming Age   121

11 End Times Implications   167

Closing Words Flattening the Mountains   185

Appendix 'A Letter to My Jewish Friends'   191

Notes   195

INTRODUCTION **A BOOK OF HOPE**

YOU ARE ABOUT TO READ A BOOK OF HOPE. This cannot always be said when we speak or write today of the people and places of the Middle East. But when we turn our eyes to God and his prophetic word, rarely do we see the world as the reporters or politicians do.

Our hope proceeds from our strong conviction that this generation is witnessing one of the most significant fulfillments of biblical prophecy outside of the physical emergence of Jesus 2000 years ago. Shockingly—maybe shamefully—much of the body of Jesus has been largely unaware of this emergent development. But if we are blind to this prophetic fulfillment, we are missing one of the greatest opportunities to participate in God's advancing of his kingdom on earth today.

The unveiling prophecy we speak of is this: the awakening of the Jewish people to the Messiah Yeshua (Jesus of Nazareth).

Does this sound strange to your ears—Jews embracing Jesus as the Messiah? It may, unless you are aware that there are more direct prophecies relating to the spiritual regeneration of the Jewish people than there were for Jesus' first coming to earth![1] Have you ever contemplated the impact it would have on our planet should an increasing number of physical Jews be transformed into spiritual leaders like Saul of Tarsus (the apostle Paul), Simon Peter, the apostle John or other New Covenant "lights?" Certainly Israel, the most contested property on earth, would take on an entirely new atmosphere should Messiah-hungry leadership like this emerge!

We believe that this is not only possible but that it is inevitable. For millennia, God's calling has rested upon the physical descendants of Abraham to be a "light unto the nations." That calling was maintained throughout the "men of old" in the Tanakh (Old Testament) and dramatically confirmed by the New Testament writers and early Jewish leadership within the church. Imagine what it might look like should the fullness of these prophecies begin to dramatically manifest itself within one of the most volatile regions on the planet!

We live in a post 9/11 world. Things will never again be as they once were. A simple and expedited check-in at the airport is a thing of the past. Many countries in the West have been plunged into a war with an unseen enemy. Daily, headlines in the world's news sources revolve around the Middle East. Compared to emergent nations like China and India, or Western powerhouses like Europe or America, the Middle East garners a disproportionate amount of media attention. Why? Because God has plans for Israel and its neighbors— plans that will culminate with not only the spiritual restoration of the Jewish people, but plans that will bring peace to the Middle East! This climactic act of divine intervention will complete the redemptive plan for earth, set in motion the moment Adam and Eve took the first bite.

This book will attempt to lay out an updated "interpretive grid" for making sense of many prophetic words and events of the Old Testament. It is not written as an academic work such as seminary professors might author, for we are attempting to communicate with the type of people we encounter in many of the places we commonly go. Yet in addition to the specific message God has encouraged us to convey here, we have relied on the excellent work of those who have gone before us, from early church fathers to many of today's leading theologians. Though this has been a challenging task, our experience has taught us that God often extends insight to widely differing camps, forcing us all into a place of humility and dependence upon him! When we hear his voice together, we hear his voice more completely, and we find a place of unified understanding—while honoring the veracity of the Scriptures and the God-fearing lineage of that "correctly handled" word of truth (2 Timothy 2:15).

Still, if you have for a long time adhered to a particular way of thinking about the end times, "something new" may unnerve your theological sensibilities. What we write may even cause you to wonder if this book could be "of God." We understand. We have wrestled with—and sometimes dismissed—alternative views of Scripture ourselves. Thus, we suggest that a cursory reading of this book will never do! You may well need to allow the passages we explore to simmer in your mind. They must be prayed over and dwelled upon. Many who believe that God is fundamentally finished with the Jewish conduit to the nations and is solely working through the church (a perspective sometimes called "replacement theology") will balk at the suggestion that God is still active in the "place" of Israel, working toward a spiritually renewed nation. Others who believe in a prophesied return to a physical "place" called Israel may hesitate at the idea of a massive spiritual revival coming to Israel outside of a tribulation period. At first glance, it may appear that this theological chasm is too wide to cross. But, as God said through the prophet Isaiah some 2,700 years ago, "...now I declare new things; before they spring forth I proclaim them to you.....therefore behold, I will once again deal marvelously with this people, wondrously marvelous..."

This book is hopeful because it counts on the progressive unveiling of God's work in the world to train our eyes to see the increasing fulfillment of his prophecies. And it is hopeful because we believe this unveiling makes room again for a unity of believers—both Jews and Gentiles—that vanished long ago from the body of Christ and has too frequently been replaced by fear and hatred on both sides. In the early days of the church of Christ, the Holy Spirit was poured out on Jews and Gentiles both—"there is no difference" (Romans 3:22). Certainly, God has not changed!

SOME NOTES FOR READING THIS BOOK

Because words often arrive at their present meanings pre-loaded in ways that writers can do little about, we find it necessary to offer several explanations before we begin.

'Yeshua' and 'Jesus.' We know that we have both Jewish and Gentile readers of this book, so we have chosen not to settle on the use of either *Yeshua* or *Jesus* to refer to our Savior. Rather, we use the names alternately, trying to employ the name that seems to fit best in each instance. We hope that we are in no way birthing offense by honoring the traditions of both audiences of readers. We similarly try to share uses of *Messiah* and *Christ* (or even *Messiah* and *the Messiah*). We also share uses of *Yahweh* and *God* (sometimes written here, as in many Bible translations, as LORD). Finally, while some Jewish readers are accustomed to seeing the name of *G-d* written incompletely, so as to prevent the defacing of his name, we will use the contemporary full form, again hoping that no offense is taken.

'Chosen people.' Many of our Messianic Jewish friends are no longer comfortable with the wording "chosen people," because it can suggest an air of superiority that they do not wish to convey. We appreciate and respect this position, particularly because of its beautiful motivation. When we use the term "chosen people" in this book, we do so because it fits the context of the words of Scripture and because we intend to present an intentional deference to the Jewish people in this book. We believe the Jews *are* especially chosen, the natural branches ahead of those of us who have been grafted in. However, to strike a balance, we sometimes alternately use phrasings like "the people of God's choice," knowing along with our Messianic friends that in full truth all who are in Christ have been chosen by God as his own.

'Anti-Semitism.' While technically the Semitic ethnicity includes all who descended from Abraham——either through Isaac or Ishmael, and either through Jacob or Esau——the current flow of understanding when the expression "anti-Semitism" is employed specifically refers to the Jews. We maintain that flow here when we write of anti-Semitism; it refers to the disrespect and often severe persecution of the Jewish people over the past two millennia.

'Messianic Jews' and **'Messianic movement.'** As the number of "Messianic Jews"—or Jews who believe that Yeshua of Nazareth is the promised Messiah of the Jewish prophecies—has grown, something of a movement among them has gained momentum. Not unlike the questions between Protestant denominations, some debate over certain matters of practice has arisen in this movement. These are not unimportant questions, but they are questions that need to be resolved among believing Jews themselves. We in no way wish to become entangled with discussions of the Messianic movement here. While we do employ the descriptive word "Messianic" at times in this book, we do so because it describes the belief of certain Jewish people and it fits the context where it used. At other times, we will employ a term we intend to be synonymous here: "believing Jews."

In contrast, we will use the term "non-believing Jews" to identify those Jews who do not at this time regard Yeshua as Messiah. This is not meant to suggest that these people do not believe in the God of the Tanakh. Neither is it meant to suggest that they do not believe that a Messiah is promised. Certainly they do! But in a book where several meanings might be attached to words like "Messianic," "traditional," and "believing," we must choose to land somewhere and maintain a consistent definition.

In all cases of word and phrase choices, we plead with those who would choose other meanings not to take offense. Absolutely no offense is intended.

1 THE RED DOOR

THE ANNUAL JEWISH CELEBRATION OF THE Passover commemorates one of the most remarkable events in the history of humanity. If you are unfamiliar with the accounts of this event as they are laid out in the biblical narrative of the exodus of the Hebrews from Egypt, you will be glad you spent the next few minutes discovering the wonder of God in the midst of this people.

When the LORD of the Hebrews (the God of Abraham, Isaac and Jacob) was preparing to end their centuries of punishing slavery under Egyptian pharaohs, he called a stuttering shepherd named Moses to lead the people to their freedom. Moses himself had been raised in the palace of the Egyptian ruler, but an enraged murder by his hand had sent him running for his life and added a severe lack of confidence to his character. Yet it was Moses whom God chose to return to the palace and, through the more polished words of his brother Aaron, demand of Pharaoh the release of the Hebrews.

It's rather absurd when you think about it. Here was a forgotten child of the court, walking into the palace in clothes of the field, requesting an audience with the king, and then presenting Pharaoh with a bizarre proposal: "Release your entire free-labor workforce to me. And in return, I'll give you nothing." You don't have to have a degree in mediation techniques to understand that Moses and Aaron were not going to get very far with this "request."

Pharaoh, as you or I would have done, turned them down.

In response, Moses, following God's specific instructions, enacted the first of what would be ten plagues to befall Pharaoh and the Egyptian people. He put his staff in the Nile River and the water turned to blood. To follow would come plagues of frogs, gnats, flies, disease among the livestock, boils, hail, locusts, and darkness. It's a daunting list, made all the more insulting by the fact that each of these afflicted all the people of the land except the Hebrews living there.

It was the final plague, however, that would be remembered throughout time. When Moses warned Pharaoh of this coming judgment—the ruler was still resistant to letting the Hebrew slaves go, as this would devastate his nation's economy—he announced that all of the firstborn males among the Egyptian people and their cattle would be put to death. After all that Pharaoh had seen via these pronouncements of Moses, a sense of grave foreboding must have washed over the king. But his heart was hard and he did not budge.

At the same time, Moses informed the Hebrew people that they too must prepare for this coming judgment, which would be meted out by the angel of the LORD. His instructions were these: The people were to take an unblemished lamb and slaughter it at dusk in order to share a meal with their family and neighbors. They were also to take the blood of the lamb and put it on the tops and sides of the doorframes of their homes. This blood was a sign to the angel of the LORD, who would come at midnight. These "red doors" announced this home to be a Jewish home, allowing the angel of the LORD to make a distinction between Egypt and Israel.

At midnight, after the people had eaten the meal according to the specific instructions to eat with haste and keep alert attention for the hour of escape from Egypt, the angel of the LORD came with the hand of death, and every firstborn male among the Egyptians died that night. But, as God spoke through Moses, "the blood will be a sign for you on the houses where you are; and when I see blood, I will *pass over* you" (Exodus 12:13).

There you have it, the Passover. God's hand of judgment was stayed by the application of righteous blood. It was a stunning act of preference for his beloved people that the Jewish community commemorates with joy into our own time.

MORE BLOOD

But while the blood on the Hebrew doors during that fearful night in Egypt demonstrated God's mercy for his beloved, this was only the beginning of what he intended for the world, only a shadow of the salvation that was to come.

Without outlining the full index of biblical references to blood as the instrument of atonement, we would do well to make note of two crucial themes that weave their way through the Old Testament (Tanakh) and make a dramatic reappearance in the New Testament:

- People incessantly operate outside of the instructions set forth by God through Moses in the Old Testament (or more specifically, in the Torah, or Law, of the Hebrew writings). These acts of disobedience, because they demonstrate a lack of faith in God's person and authority, are classified as sin. All people are guilty of sin.

- God's normal requirement for the atonement of sin was the blood of an animal sacrificed on an altar before Him.[2]

In the spiritual design of God, then, the blood of the sacrificed animals was intended to act as a sign to God that those offering the sacrifice were repentant and understood that forgiveness comes from God. This was not an act of *appeasement*, as we shall soon see.

With this in mind, we are compelled to examine the New Testament references to the "once for all" sacrifice made by Jesus of Nazareth, for remarkably he is established in these later writings to the Hebrews as the one whose blood now "purchases" our salvation.

The New Testament is made up chiefly of two kinds of writings. There are five historical accounts, four of those being the Gospels that tell of Jesus' life, death and resurrection, and the fifth being an account of the work of God's Spirit through the apostles of Jesus (the book of Acts). Nearly all the rest of the New Testament (not including Revelation) is comprised of letters written from the apostles to both Jewish and non-Jewish people as they considered Jesus' Messiahship and made a decision to follow him both as individuals and in church fellowships.

One letter, Hebrews, was written specifically to those of Jewish origin. While it is the one letter (or epistle) whose author does not "sign" his work, many scholars agree that it carries the style and reasoning of the many other letters written by the apostle Paul.

In the letter to the Hebrews, the writer made many connections between the Old Testament priesthood and sacrifices to the person and work of Jesus of Nazareth. These aspects of

Jesus, the writer argues, establish him as the Savior (also Messiah or Christ) that the Jewish people had so long desired. And principal among the writer's argumentation was blood. To see this, we will briefly consider three passages:

> The law is only a shadow of the good things that are coming—not the realities themselves. For this reason it can never, by the same sacrifices repeated endlessly year after year, make perfect those who draw near to worship. If it could, would they not have stopped being offered? For the worshippers would have been cleansed once for all, and would no longer have felt guilty for their sins. But those sacrifices are an annual reminder of sins, because it is impossible for the blood of bulls and goats to take away sins. (Hebrews 10:1-4)

In addition to laying out the reason that "a better sacrifice" had to come for our sake, this passage helps us understand that animal sacrifices could not *appease* God, as though he is manipulated by our actions. Rather, God chose in his plan of mercy to send his own Son, Jesus, to be that better sacrifice.

> Such a high priest meets our need—one who is holy, blameless, pure, set apart from sinners, exalted above the heavens. Unlike other high priests, he does not need to offer sacrifices day after day, first for his own sins, and then for the sins of the people. He sacrificed for their sins once for all when he offered himself. For the law appoints as high priests men who are weak; but the oath, which came after the law, appointed the Son, who has been made perfect forever. (Hebrews 7:26-28)

What a wonder is being presented here! Jesus not only was acting in the line of the ancient priests, but he served as well in the place of the ancient sacrifices. The Son of God was assigned by God to fulfill completely the law of God. And the next passage clarifies the means by which Jesus, the Son of God, did this.

> He did not enter by means of the blood of goats and calves; but he entered the Most Holy Place once for all by his own blood, having obtained eternal redemption. The blood of goats and bulls and the ashes of a heifer sprinkled on those who are ceremonially unclean sanctify them so that they are outwardly clean. How much more, then, will the blood of Christ [Jesus], who through the eternal Spirit offered himself unblemished to God, cleanse our consciences from acts that lead to death, so that we may serve the living God! (Hebrews 9:12-14)

So there it is. The red door of Passover remains. Without the blood of Jesus, there is no passage into salvation. Jesus himself called this door "narrow." Indeed, it is narrow in the sense that it may only be passed through when we recognize his blood, believe in its power to save, and live by faith in the one who shed it. Only then will the God of Abraham, Isaac, and Jacob, the same God who rescued the Hebrews from the Egyptians, "pass over" us in judgment and apply to us the love he has for his Son.

2 THE RED DOOR COMMUNITY

IF THE BLOOD OF JESUS IS APPLIED TO THE DOOR of our lives, allowing us to live under the grace and mercy of God, we are led to ask ourselves questions of stunning significance, especially in our time. We might do best to begin with this one: *What does this mean in terms of religion?*

Because of the surveys of world religion that most people have experienced throughout their school years, and because of the generalized play given to the major world religions in most media references, many people hold to the understanding that religions are only sets of beliefs that sometimes complement and sometimes oppose one another. For this reason, many people recognize Jesus as an insightful teacher or even the founder of a dominant world religion. But they are unaware of the Bible's teachings that Jesus is:

- the Son of the Creator God
- the perfect sacrifice made for our sins
- the priest who intercedes between sinful people and the holy God
- the only provision of God through which we may come into a saved and eternal relationship with him

Of course, those who do not wish to accept the biblical line of reasoning will find grounds for contention here. Sadly, these would be those who miss the good news that lies within such a religion-busting set of facts. There is so much comfort in the fact that we *cannot* do it on our own, in the admission that every set of legalistic religious standards in the world is beyond the capability of any person to obey. There is so much comfort in the fact that we *cannot* appease God. What the Bible teaches is that our salvation can come only through a Savior, the Messiah promised in the Old Testament and delivered by God in the first century (as recounted in the pages of the New Testament).

What this means above all else is that religion is set aside in favor of one man, Jesus Christ. He did not come to *found* a religion, but to *find* men and women who were truly interested in turning their spirits (or hearts) over to God.[3]

Who are these people and where do they come from?

The apostle Paul, a once contentious enemy of Jesus who was plucked from among the Jewish leadership to carry the news of Jesus to the Gentiles in a stunning turn of events, wrote these words:

> **We preach Christ crucified: a stumbling block to Jews and foolishness to Gentiles, but to those whom God has called, both Jews and Greeks, Christ the power of God and the wisdom of God,[4]**

and also these:

> **There is neither Jew nor Greek, slave nor free, male nor female, for you are all one in Christ Jesus.[5]**

In other words, the Bible tells us that Jesus Christ—and

particularly the act of his crucifixion——both repels and welcomes people.

Some will regard the fact that he sacrificially gave his life on that cross as an absurdity. They see neither a point in this action, nor power in it. They are united in their unbelief of Jesus' role as priest and sacrifice.

Others, though, find the fulfillment of an ancient promise——that God will send a Savior (Messiah) for his people——in the crucifixion. They understand the prophecies of the Old Testament and the Gospel accounts of the life, death and resurrection of Jesus of Nazareth to be knit together over time——the words of God fulfilled by his actions. These people are united in their belief in the power of Jesus' blood to cleanse them of their sin and save them from eternal death. These people, we might say, make up the Red Door Community.

Which all sounds well and good, even idealistic. After all, isn't this most everyone's concept of God——the one who unifies people of all kinds under his watchful eye and purpose?

But to the embarrassment of all who read the Bible with intensity, the history of our planet since the time of Jesus has left us with this strong impression: "Jews" and "Christians" are not only in different camps, but those camps have frequently been at war——if not physically, then ideologically.

Many Jewish leaders since the time of Paul have argued that Jesus is not the promised Messiah of the Hebrew prophecies and that those who say he is are leading people away from the God of Abraham, Isaac and Jacob. At times these arguments have led to false accusations, violence, even murder. Those in Israel today who teach that Yeshua (Jesus) is the Messiah find themselves targeted for persecution by ultra-orthodox Jewish factions.[6]

But Christians are not guiltless. They, too, have through the centuries staged bloody battles against Jewish households and neighborhoods. Cries of "Christ killers," designed to demean Jewish people in the basest of ways, have led to deep divisions between "the chosen people" (Hebrews/Jews in the Old Testament) and "those whom God has called" (all believers of Jesus in the New Testament).[7]

Of course, there are those of both people, Jew and Gentile alike, who would say that extreme people and extreme actions do not speak for them. And there is historical evidence that this is true; a few renegades acting outside of the prevailing counsel of the time have more than once made a bad name for everyone. Likewise, some who have been categorized as "Christian" but have in no way acted like Christ have committed infamous offenses against the Jewish people.

As authors, we are firmly convinced that we would do best as co-believers in Jesus the Messiah, Jewish or Gentile, to understand how rich our co-heritage is. For we can trace this heritage back much farther even than the cross of Christ. We can find "types and shadows" throughout the Old Testament Jewish writings that God's plan has always allowed an open door for joint purpose and joint ministry among *all* who are united in Christ.

It is the design of the ensuing pages of this book to explore the past, present and future of The Red Door Community as laid out in Scripture. While The Red Door Community may be a moniker of our own wording for our own time, its existence among the accounts of the Bible is undeniable. And when we see the thread of Christ's atoning work for us and how this thread unites those who lean wholly on him for their eternal life, we cannot help but praise the Living God of all people.

What a privilege it is for us to lift such praise! What a hope it is of ours that you will join us with joy!

3 THE GENTILE TEST

EVERY BOOK IS WRITTEN WITH A PARTICULAR audience in mind. While we take great delight in standing with our believing Jewish brothers and sisters in Yeshua, and we would be pleased if they find many blessings in this book, our work will best be accomplished here if we are allowed to usher our Gentile readers into an understanding of the community of faith that needs to exist between them and their Jewish co-heirs in the kingdom of God.

In order to do this, we intend to put our Gentile friends to a bit of a test in this chapter. It is a test of knowledge and of affiliation. And we believe it will give you an increased sense of your own heart in this matter of Gentiles and Jews united.

THE TESTS OF KNOWLEDGE

Allow us to begin by asking a straightforward question: *What do non-Jews owe to those who are Jewish?*

It may never have occurred to you that Gentiles owe Jews anything. Of course, there are many people in the world to whom you may think you owe no debt. In a material sense, this may be accurate. In the sense of the "brotherhood of humanity," however, most of us understand that we owe each person whatever must be granted to them for the sake of their dignity, just as we would desire from others. Beyond this, as followers of Christ, we owe each person the very expressions of grace that Christ has shown to us. Though we cannot deliver these in the same way that Jesus did (and still does), we must make every attempt to dispense forgiveness and display mercy, intercede with God for those too weak or too blind to do this themselves, patiently endure the falsehoods and evil actions of others, and generally render love in whatever way most reflects our Lord. These things we owe to Jews and Gentiles alike.

But there is also a debt of gratitude that Gentiles must be aware of when entering into conversation and relationship with Jewish people, whether or not they are believers in Yeshua. It is a debt of gratitude based on God-given positions and roles that the Jewish people have borne through history. These have served to create a spiritual lineage that continues to us now. Consider:

The Abrahamic Blessing. In the twelfth chapter of Genesis, we are amazed to discover that of all the people living on the planet at the time, God initiated a relationship with Abram, who lived in Ur of the Chaldeans. So little is known of Abram's life before the call of God that we stand no chance of making a case for Abram's merit in God's approaching him. Simply, God chose Abram. Eventually, God would direct Abram to change his name from Abram (meaning "exalted father") to Abraham (meaning "father of many"), and thus the original promise God gave to Abram in Genesis 12:2-3 is known as the Abrahamic covenant. It reads like this: "I will make you into a great nation and I will bless you; I will make your name great, and you will be a blessing. I will bless those who bless you, and whoever curses you, I will curse, and all the people on earth will be blessed through you."

To begin, then, we can say that all non-Jews owe a debt to the Jewish people in deference to God's sovereign choice of the Jewish people as his conduit for blessing. It is a debt of honor, both to the Lord, who chose the Jewish descendants of Abraham, and to the Jews themselves as those people of his choice.

The Squeeze of Persecution. We would not be wrong to say that God's blessing through time has been poured through an upside-down funnel. That is, it began with a very small group of people and only later, after the coming of the Messiah, spread widely to the rest of the world. However, the time that the blessing remained in the small part of the spout spanned millennia, and even into our time, the people there—the Jews— have received the greatest attention and the greatest abuse. For their adherence to the idea of One True God and to a specific moral code handed down by that God, the Jewish people have endured recurring and extreme persecution; they have been the target of tyrants, bullies, and bigots.

Adherence to a particular God or a particular form of faith, however, does not differentiate the Jewish people from many of the people of history and geography. Indeed, their cultural customs and social priorities are in many ways similar to some of the most successful and respected nations throughout time. We would have to argue that the Jewish people have likely been persecuted so widely and so severely for spiritual reasons, particularly if we hold to the biblical truth that "our struggle is not against flesh and blood, but against the rulers, against the authorities, against the powers of this dark world and against the spiritual forces of evil in the heavenly realms."[8]

Consider, for instance, that the persecution of the Jews may be for these reasons:

- The seed of the woman that would crush Satan's head would be of Jewish descent. The Jews are warred against because they carry the bloodline of salvation for all people.

- The Jewish people cry out for the Messiah. Those who believe that he is Yeshua cry as well with praise, "Blessed is he who comes in the name of the LORD!"

- The enemy would love to thwart the second coming of the Messiah. If, as we will discuss in later chapters, a Jewish revival will precede this earthly return of the Savior, the enemy may be convinced that he can prevent this return by eliminating all Jews. As there are rulers in the world today who have announced their desire for this very thing——the complete elimination of the Jews[9]——it is not far-fetched to suggest that an effort is being made through these leaders by the enemy of salvation, Satan, to persecute and kill all Jews.

Still, the Jewish people endure in the faithfulness of God. And they should, for God promised such through Isaiah when he announced, "As the new heavens and the new earth that I make will endure before me, so will your name and descendants endure."[10]

For this reason, we who follow the progression of the faith as passed down through the Messiah owe the Jewish people a debt of compassion. We must recognize their unwanted role as the target of derision and violence, and respond with apology for the sins of our own Gentile predecessors, seeking forgiveness and making restitution if possible, even in small ways. Jews who recognize authentic words of compassionate contrition from Gentile believers are placed in a position of responding to the grace of Christ in the same way that we were ourselves when we were saved in him![11]

The Care of the Word. Here is a third vital piece of knowledge Gentiles must remember as we turn a caring eye toward the Jewish people: for centuries, they alone were the guardians of the Word of God (the Bible). While some particular men—prophets, kings, and poets—received the words of God and recorded them as directed by the Lord, others—scribes and priests—were given the enduring responsibility of regenerating those words in written form and teaching them in verbal form, so that the generations to follow would have access to the same histories, psalms and prophecies upon which our faith in God is learned and advanced.

Certainly, as believers in the promised Messiah, who is Jesus, we should understand the importance of being able to trace a prophetic progression to Jesus, showing that our worship of this man from Nazareth is not based simply on the excellent earthly works of a notable historical figure, but rather it is the worship of the Son of God, whose advent and life were pronounced in detailed prophecies written hundreds of years before his earthly birth.[12] The recording and protection of these sacred words rested in the hands of the Jewish men whose job it was to write them down and recopy them faithfully. For this, we owe the Jewish people a debt of deep appreciation for the "living and active" Word of God as it has been handed down to us.

If you are a non-Jew who understands and relishes these blessings that have been delivered to us through the Jewish people, you are on your way to passing "the Gentile test." You are prepared to stand with the Jewish people, both those who have yet to recognize Yeshua as Messiah and those who have already been given "eyes to see and ears to hear" and have placed their trust in the Savior. But we think it is also extremely important that you know you are not alone in such support of the Jews.

A LINEAGE OF CROSSOVER

While as Gentiles, we can retrace our steps to the seeds of God's saving plan back through the Jewish people, we think you will also be excited to find that Scripture includes reference to many people throughout time who came to faith in the God of Abraham, Isaac and Jacob from outside of the ethnic boundaries. At least one popular theological system of the last century established suggested "constraints" for when God would do his work through certain people, which has led some to mistakenly believe that there was a time for the Jews, and there is now time for the Gentiles, without crossover. This simply is not the case. The fact that God has united Jews and Gentiles under his Son Jesus Christ is simply an expansion of notable cases of Gentiles who have "passed the test" and united themselves with the Jewish people throughout time. Let's investigate some important examples:

Caleb. Although we are prepared to offer a number of examples of Gentiles whose hearts were turned to the heart and people of the LORD of the Jews, none rings with the wonder of Caleb the Kenizzite. Caleb's participation with Joshua as one of the two faithful leaders among the band of spies sent into the land of Canaan has been loudly trumpeted in the modern church, where we love our heroes. What has hardly been whispered, however, is that Caleb was not Jewish by birth. Rather, he was the son of Jephunneh the Kenizzite (Numbers 32:12). Little is known about the origin of the Kenizzites, except that they do not occur in the lineages of the Jews. Caleb descended from a Gentile family, perhaps brought into the Jewish fold through marriage. What is remarkable to remember is that it was Caleb the Gentile (whose very name meant "dog," a common insult between Jews and Arabs of the region) and Joshua the Jew who survived the exodus generation out of Egypt to cross the Jordan River into the Promised Land——only these two men! How fitting that God would unite Jew and Gentile in leading his people into their original earthly land, then millennia later inspire Paul to write that Jew and Gentile had become "one new man" in Christ, as the age of the church was ushered in. [13]

Rahab. We are not the first to observe that God's ways are often absurdly different from our own. In particular, he has frequently chosen the unlikeliest people to serve him throughout history. Rahab of Jericho was such a person: a woman, a reputed prostitute, and a Gentile. Yet it was this woman who harbored Israel's spies in the city. For her aid she was protected when the invasion of the city was enacted, and for her faith she was lauded by the New Testament writers of Hebrews and James.

Ruth. A second Gentile woman, Ruth, acted with such faith in the God of the Jews that an entire Old Testament book was committed to the accounts of her life. Set aside a few minutes to read this fascinating little book, and you will be moved both by the woman's faithfulness, and by the Hebrew community's willingness to fold her in as well. They recognized in her the servant's heart that reveals true faith, and they blessed her with the blessings of God. Indeed, Ruth's life serves as a metaphor of the salvation we all may receive through the "kinsman-re-deemer" who is our Savior, Jesus.

Other Old Testament examples. While the cases of Caleb, Rahab, and Ruth bear special significance and their faith in the One True God is especially recognized in Scripture, others outside the Jewish bloodlines crossed over in faith to believe. These included the widow of Zaraphath who recognized Elijah as a prophet of God and served him as such (1 Kings 17:7-24); Naaman the Aramean military commander who was healed of leprosy and praised God, saying, "Now I know that there is no God in all the world except in Israel" (2 Kings 5:1-19); and Nebuchadnezzar, king of Babylon, whose idolatry was turned to belief when God exiled the king to a year living like the cows of the field, eating grass and enduring exposure (Daniel 4).

As we move from the Old Testament to the New, where Jesus engages a number of Gentiles—sometimes at his initiation and sometimes at theirs—you will notice that there is a certain directness to Jesus' prodding. He wants to know whether these are Gentiles who are looking for a miracle for their own physical sake, or whether they possess a real understanding of how God loves the Jewish people and that salvation to the world comes through them. When Jesus discovers this kind of deference in a Gentile, his reaction is overwhelmingly positive; he praises the faith of the Gentile and offers his blessing. This is the essence of what we are calling "the Gentile Test": *Do you recognize that salvation is from the Jews?* Although Jesus' own interaction with Gentiles was limited, he nearly always went right to this point with them. And if their faith made it evident that they did recognize this progression of God's favor, so to speak, Jesus' own excitement was clear in his words and his actions.

The Magi. The accounts of Jesus' childhood as they are recorded in the Gospel of Matthew include the visit of the Magi, or wise men, about two years after Jesus' birth. These Magi had traveled "from the east" to worship Jesus, whose star they had recognized in the sky. Every tradition surrounding this account places the origin of the Magi well to the east of Bethlehem, far outside the realm of Israel. In other words, these first worshippers of Jesus were not Jewish but Gentile! The interaction these men had with King Herod included their reference to Micah's Messianic prophecy that a shepherd for God's people would arise from Bethlehem. Not only did these Gentile wise men pass the Gentile test by recognizing that salvation would come from the Jews, but they were the first apart from Jesus' mother (and perhaps Joseph, her husband) to understand that Jesus, born in Bethlehem, was the fulfillment of the Messianic prophecies and that very salvation.

The woman at the well. Another powerful New Testament story involves the Samaritan woman at the well in John 4. While the Samaritans possessed some Hebrew blood, they were regarded as half-breeds and heretics by the Jews themselves; Jewish men would have nothing to do with Samaritan women especially. Yet Jesus initiated a conversation with this woman, and when he revealed to her that he knew all about her sordid past but had life to offer her all the same, she turned her heart of faith to him. She did this despite the fact that Jesus clearly told her that "salvation is from the Jews" (verse 22). Because she was looking for the Messiah, she was able and willing to recognize the remarkable mantle of authority upon Jesus. Not only did the woman's testimony demonstrate her belief, but "many of the Samaritans from that town believed because of" it. In this way, we might say that not only did the Samaritan woman pass the Gentile test, but she led the local study group!

The Roman centurion. Jesus was Jewish. And he was clear that his purpose in coming was to interact with the Jews. But more than once he was taken aback by the faith of non-Jewish people he encountered. One such case was the Roman centurion who approached him while he was in Capernaum. This man sought healing for his gravely ill servant. Jesus was coaxed into meeting with the man by some religious leaders who thought they "owed" the centurion a favor. Why? Because this Gentile had been so good to the Jews—"he loves our nation and has built our synagogue." What we find, however, was that the centurion was also a man of intense faith. He told Jesus that he recognized Jesus' authority as akin to his own as a military commander: tell someone to do something, and it would be done. Jesus praised the centurion, saying, "I tell you, I have not found such great faith even in Israel."[14] The servant was healed.

The Canaanite woman. Similarly, Jesus was approached by a woman of great faith when he was near Tyre. This woman, a native Canaanite, begged Jesus to free her daughter from demon possession. Jesus was stand-offish, saying that he had been sent "only to the lost sheep of the house of Israel." He was testing her resolve, yes, but also her understanding of the covenantal order of God's kingdom. The woman passed the test, for she was certainly willing in this sense to "give honor where honor is due." Rather than turning away at Jesus' hesitance to assist her, she pleaded with him and said, "Even the dogs eat the crumbs that fall from their masters' table."[15] Again, Jesus was amazed, declaring her to be a woman of great faith, and her daughter was healed in that hour.

Cornelius. Up to this first century point in history, the out-flow through that upside-down funnel of blessing moved very slowly through the narrow top that was the Jewish people. But through another Roman centurion, the logjam was about to break; Jewish believers were going to be challenged and en-couraged to welcome all who were not Israel in blood but true Israel in faith. That centurion was a man named Cornelius, a resident of Caesarea. In a dream, God revealed to the unoffi-cial leader of the apostles, Peter, that the door to salvation was about to be opened to the Gentiles. Peter could never have imagined such a possibility before this time, but the dream was so clear, and the developments after the dream were so immediate, that Peter could not deny the dream's authenticity. He went to meet with Cornelius, a man who was "devout and God-fearing," giving generously and praying regularly—traits for which he was "respected by all the Jewish people." A case could be made that Cornelius was the prime Gentile candi-date for the salvation of Jesus Christ and the baptism of the Holy Spirit, as he had already passed the Gentile test of know-ing, respecting and serving the Jews. In the hour that followed their meeting, Peter preached the Good News of Christ to the many who were assembled in Cornelius' house, and "the circumcised (Jewish) believers who had come with Peter were astonished that the gift of the Holy Spirit had been poured out *even on the Gentiles*" (emphasis added). In the aftermath of this stunning event, Peter explained the occurrences to the Jewish believers in Jerusalem, the Holy Spirit confirmed the truth of his accounts in the hearts of his listeners, and the community of Yeshua "praised God, saying, 'So then, God has granted even the Gentiles repentance unto life.'"[16]

THE BROAD REACH OF THE MESSIAH

Jesus recognized that his death, resurrection and the ensuing coming of the Holy Spirit as the ongoing intercessor between God and man would usher in a unity of belief that included Jews and Gentiles. In the final week of his life, a group of Greeks came to Jerusalem to worship God. They also requested an audience with Jesus. When the disciples delivered this request, Jesus replied in a way that must have seemed entirely illogical to the disciples at that time. He said: "The hour has come for the Son of Man to be glorified. I tell you the truth, unless a kernel of wheat falls to the ground and dies, it remains only a single seed. But if it dies, it produces many seeds."[17] Jesus knew that his death, in keeping with God's ongoing purposes for his Son's life and for the reconciliation of the world, would open the door for many to believe——including those, like these Greeks, not of Jewish descent. The disciples would carry the Messianic witness to the world. Indeed, Jesus would actually present himself to Jews and Gentiles everywhere through his disciples, both those who had walked with him when he was on earth and those who follow and bear witness to him now. Much of the remainder of this book is given over to the discussion of this witness as it is made by Jewish and Gentile believers united in the Messiah.

Still, if we are Gentiles, we should be very aware that the saving work of Jesus was never intended to strip the Jews of their special place in God's heart. They remain the apple of his eye, and those who touch the Jews touch God's endeared ones (Zechariah 2:8). It is imperative for us, then, to be gentle and reconciliatory with our touch. We are, in the spirit of Christ, to be ministers and healers, not combatants or cursers, as some of our forebears have been. When our hearts are turned in this compassionate direction, we have passed the Gentile test, joining the lineage of history's appreciators, those who have loved the Jewish people as God has loved them.

But as the next chapter explains, we have an even greater lineage to discover. It is the lineage of faith that began with the Jews and continues only through them, as long as they are rooted and growing in the Messiah.

THE CHAPTER IN REVIEW

The Gentile Test

ONE BIG IDEA

All Gentiles draw their spiritual lineage through the Jewish people. Therefore, all Gentiles can expect to be 'tested' as to their appreciation of God's work among the Jews.

KEY POINTS

• *Gentiles should find appreciation and show respect for the Jewish people because of God's blessing on and through Abraham, the history of persecution against the Jewish people, and the Jewish care for God's Word (Scripture).*

• *Righteous understanding of God's own Jewish focus was demonstrated by many key Gentiles in both the Old and New Testaments. Among those were Caleb, Rahab, and Ruth in the Old Testament, and the Magi, the woman at the well, the confident Roman centurion, the Canaanite woman, and Cornelius in the New Testament.*

• *While the work of Jesus on the cross opened the door of salvation for all people, both Jewish and non-Jewish, this work was never intended to remove the Jews from their special place in God's heart. Those who recognize this will interact with the Jewish people favorably, knowing they are the apple of God's eye.*

4 NATURAL AND WILD TOGETHER

IN THE HEART OF CENTRAL CALIFORNIA, TOURISTS with curious eyes will find the unique Forestiere Underground Gardens. In 1906 a Sicilian immigrant named Baldassare Forestiere began work on a labor of love that eventually spanned 40 years of commitment. Into 10 acres of fertile ground in the San Joaquin Valley, he dug a series of tunnels and recesses fashioned after the catacombs of ancient Rome. Above ground and below, Forestiere planted trees of all kinds, demonstrating the fruit of an attentive tender's care.

But the masterpiece amongst Forestiere's work was a single tree that stood in a below-surface courtyard. Using the process of grafting, by which a living branch from one tree is cut into the stalk of another tree, the farmer created a single tree that produced seven different varieties of citrus!

Though Forestiere's intent may not have been theological, his remarkable tree provides a beautiful picture of the purposes of God in relation to Jews, Gentiles and salvation, as outlined by the apostle Paul in his letter to the Romans.

If you are one of those Gentiles we spoke of in the last chapter, one whose heart passes the test of love for the Jewish people, you will want to become increasingly versed in the passages of Romans that establish the interwoven relationship of faith that exists between the natural branches that are the Jews and the ingrafted branches that are the Gentiles. This chapter, then, is set aside to help trace that vital relationship, which is made possible only through the common Savior, who is Jesus.

THE HERITAGE OF ISRAEL

When we use the term "Israel" today, we run the risk of stirring up political concerns among those who follow the ever-developing news in the Middle East, where Jews, Muslims, Christians, and secularists of all political persuasions reside alongside one another and participate in the sometimes violent outworkings of their differences.

Biblically, there were also times when the term "Israel" referred to this strip of land on the eastern edge of the Mediterranean Sea. Always, however, Israel referred to a specific group of people, those descended from Abraham, then through his son Isaac (not Ishmael) and Isaac's son Jacob (not Esau). It was Jacob who was renamed Israel (meaning "he struggles with God") after a noted wrestling match with God, as described in Genesis 32.

In Paul's letter to the Romans, he was referring to the people of Israel, those whose descendancy came through Abraham, Isaac and Jacob. For the most part in Paul's time, these people did dwell in the same geographic land we now call Israel. However, for our discussion at this particular stage, we are, with Paul, interested in *Israel the people* as opposed to *Israel the land* (the latter discussion coming in ensuing chapters).

Let's begin with the heritage carried through the Jewish people, to which we alluded in the last chapter, where we talked of the Jewish role in the Abrahamic blessing and the care of the Word of God. Here are Paul's far more inclusive words about the heritage of the Jewish people:

> For I could wish that I myself were cursed and cut off
> from Christ for the sake of my brothers, those of my
> own race, the people of Israel. Theirs is the adoption as
> sons; theirs the divine glory, the covenants, the receiving
> of the law, the temple worship and the promises. Theirs
> are the patriarchs, and from them is traced the an-
> cestry of Christ, who is God over all, forever praised!
> Amen. (Romans 9:3-5)

Paul's heart for the Jewish people was so great that he expressed a willingness to surrender his security and his relationship with Christ in order that they might receive salvation
through Jesus. Why would he do this? Because he knew from
their heritage that God desired the hearts of these people. God,
Paul was writing, had given the Jewish people every advantage.
As God's, they had seen his glory and been made children of
his promises. Moreover, they had been given the very instruction of God, passed down to them through leaders of faith and
devotion. And then there was this: Jesus himself, the one Paul
was proclaiming as the promised Messiah, was Jewish!

We are always surprised to find amazement among Gentiles
that Jews would believe that Jesus is the Messiah, their Savior.
Is it strange that Jewish people would believe and follow a Jewish man who lived according to Jewish law as their Jewish Messiah? Certainly it is far stranger that non-Jews would believe
and follow such a Jewish man!

The heritage from which Jesus came was decidedly Jewish.
And yet Paul wrote that the Messiah had come and that his
own people had missed him:

> What then shall we say? That the Gentiles, who did
> not pursue righteousness, have obtained it, a righ-
> teousness that is by faith; but Israel, who pursued a

> law of righteousness, has not attained it. Why not?
> Because they pursued it not by faith but as if it were
> by works. They stumbled over the "stumbling stone."
> (Romans 9:30-32)[18]

By referring to the Old Testament prophecies of Psalm 118 and Isaiah 8 that speak of this stumbling, Paul was showing that God had foreseen this tragic rejection of Yeshua as the Messiah all along. Although the letter to the Romans has long been revered as one of ancient writing's most ambitious pieces of cogent argumentation, Paul was not laying out a line of argumentation here. He was laying out his heart, which was broken for his ethnic brothers and sisters, the Jewish people. Shouldn't our hearts, aligned with our brother Paul, break in the same way?

FAITH, THE ESSENTIAL COMPONENT

However, Paul knew that his compassionate heart would not save these people, not even if it were expressed in a cosmic bargain—his soul for theirs. No righteousness of our own, Paul repeatedly expressed, can bring salvation. True righteousness comes only through faith in the one who was fully righteous, Yeshua, the Messiah.

This message did not rest well with most Jews in Paul's time; it does not rest well with most Jews now. Paul quoted the prophet Isaiah, who relayed the words of God to the Jews: "All day long I have held out my hands to a disobedient and obstinate people" (Isaiah 65:2, quoted in Romans 10:21).

But there was a remnant of faith, a group of Jews in Paul's time that included the apostles and several thousand others, who were moved to belief in Jesus. We read in the early chapters of the book of Acts that their numbers increased daily.

They had found their Messiah. For this, Paul was exceedingly glad. Among them, Jesus did "find faith on the earth."

This group of believing Jews continues today, and we look forward to introducing them to you in chapter 6. First, however, we must note that the prevailing belief among Jewish people is that Jesus was not Messiah. And yet, Paul found a reason for this "hardening" of the Jews that should humble every Gentile believer:

> Again I ask: Did they stumble so as to fall beyond recovery? Not at all! Rather, because of their transgression, salvation has come to the Gentiles to make Israel envious. (Romans 11:11)

That is, there is an amazing purpose in the salvation of the Gentiles. We are being used by God to capture the hearts of his people once again. There is a "fullness" yet to come for the Jews, and those who are not Jewish have been saved that this fullness might occur:

> But if their transgression means riches for the world, and their loss means riches for the Gentiles, how much greater riches will their fullness bring!...
> For if their rejection is the reconciliation of the world, what will their acceptance be but life from the dead? (Romans 11:12, 15)

God has marvelous plans still to come for the Jewish people. In the meantime, those of us who are not Jewish must exercise a humble compassion toward the Jews, who are suffering the very things we were suffering when we were living a life apart from the saving work of Jesus.

THE WILD OLIVE SHOOT

Sadly, throughout history, non-Jewish religious leaders have fallen into the sin of spiritual pride when assessing the Jewish condition. A humble awareness of Romans 11 should have been enough to keep hurtful words and actions from arising out of the Gentile camp. It was not. Early Christian codes targeted Jews in their restrictions and laws; some renegade Crusaders used the might at their disposal to make unauthorized but brutal forays against Jews in Europe; notoriously, Martin Luther wrote ill of the Jews in his book *On the Jews and Their Lies*. Yes, at times apologetic arguments against Judaism's theology have perhaps been wrongly categorized as anti-Semitism; but at other times these same arguments have been commandeered to justify injurious action against people of Jewish descent. In the wake of such atrocities, as well as those performed by despots such as Adolf Hitler, we should be quick to express our sorrow, or shame, and our deepest apologies to the Jewish people. Indeed, if you are truly serious about softening the heart of a Jewish friend, begin with a face-to-face expression of regret for the horrors that have plagued the Jewish people throughout history.

But in addition to regret, we must understand the gratitude about which Paul wrote to the Romans, a non-Jewish people who needed an education about their own place before God. Let's look at the core passage that should spark this gratitude, and evaluate what the components of its metaphor mean:

> If some of the branches have been broken off, and you, though a wild olive shoot, have been grafted in among the others and now share in the nourishing sap from the olive root, do not boast over those branches. If you do, consider this: You do not support the root,

but the root supports you. You will say then, "Branches were broken off so I could be grafted in." Granted. But they have been broken off because of unbelief, and you stand by faith. Do not be arrogant, but be afraid. For if God did not spare the natural branches, he will not spare you either.

Consider therefore the kindness and sternness of God: sternness to those who fell, but kindness to you, provided that you continue in his kindness. Otherwise, you will be cut off. And if they do not persist in unbelief, they will be grafted in, for God is able to graft them in again. After all, if you were cut out of an olive tree that is wild by nature, and contrary to nature were grafted into a cultivated olive tree, how much more readily will these, the natural branches, be grafted into their own olive tree! (Romans 11:17-24)

Paul paints a picture crucial to us, be we Jew or Gentile. For in this passage we both find our place.

The Jews of old grew from the root of God the Father. Their life depended on his strength. They were "cultivated" by him to be the people of his promise.

Unfortunately, we discover in our reading of the Old Testament histories and the words of the Old Testament prophets that as the generations progressed, many Jewish people abandoned the faith of their ancestors, both in heart and in action. Without faith, no one can remain connected to God, and thus, these people were "broken off," separated from the life source that was meant to sustain them.

However, God's plan held far wider promise than originally believed. Through Christ, those who were not Jewish were being welcomed into the "garden of God," if they came by faith in Jesus as the promised Messiah. When any Gentile made such an expression and commitment of faith, Paul told the Romans, it was as though they were grafted in to the living tree of Christ, *alongside* those Jews who already believed in him.

We cannot overstate the importance of this truth. It is not as though there are two faiths, one Jewish and one Gentile, in the one true God. Rather, where are those who believe that only faith in the one who was truly righteous (Yeshua) is credited as the righteousness that brings salvation? Such people are nourished by the root of his love. Jewish ethnicity or non-Jewish ethnicity is of no saving value. Adherence to the Mosaic law or non-adherence to the Mosaic law is of no saving value. Salvation is available only through Yeshua, the Son of God, the promised Messiah.

The knowledge of this fact should arrest any pride on either side. Life is in Christ. Paul warned the Gentiles regarding their possession of a place in God's kingdom: "Do not be arrogant, but be afraid." Some Jews had rejected the way of faith and lost their position with God; the same could be said of Gentiles. The minute we start depending on our heritage or our moral code or our relative goodness over and above others, we have surrendered the place of faith in the saving work of Christ. We, too, would find ourselves separated from the living tree.

There is another reason for Gentiles to remain most humble about the grace that has come their way: a Jewish person is no more trapped in unbelief than a Gentile; many Jews will come to believe in Jesus, gaining life again, grafted back into the living tree.

For both Jews and Gentiles, salvation remains the highest impetus for celebration in heaven and on earth. Jesus himself spoke of the joy that arises in heaven when a sinner repents. Who is a sinner? Anyone who is trapped in the unbelief toward Jesus that requires instead a dependence on one's own works to gain God's attention. Such a dependence denies the saving work of Jesus. But when a person rejects his or her own works, turns from the sin of unbelief, and trusts wholly in salvation through Christ's blood and grace, there is reason to celebrate——Jews for Jews, Jews for Gentiles, Gentiles for Jews, and Gentiles for Gentiles. For then, there really is "neither Jew nor Greek...for all are one in Christ Jesus."[19] Jesus really has created "in himself one new man out of the two."[20]

As Baldassare Forestiere would have enjoyed telling us, the life of the branch, whether natural or grafted-in, is only as healthy as the life of the tree. There is health in the tree, which is the Messiah. Moreover, the number of natural branches being grafted back into Messiah is increasing in our own time, as more and more Jewish men and women are awakened to Yeshua, the Jewish Savior. But who are these people, and how can we rejoice in our co-existence with them as believers? We will explore the answer to that question in chapter 6, after we briefly explain our approach to the prophetic passages that help advance our understanding of the growing relationship between Jewish and Gentile believers.

THE CHAPTER IN REVIEW

Natural and Wild Together

ONE BIG IDEA

After the coming of the Holy Spirit at Pentecost, God intended that Jews and Gentiles would grow together in the community of faith in the Messiah. Still, as Paul wrote to the Romans, the original covenants of God were made with the Jewish people.

KEY POINTS

• God desires the hearts of the Jewish people. The desires of God's heart should be the desires of our hearts.

• Faith in Jesus is the essential component that bonds us with God and with one another as we worship God.

• The history of Christendom has been riddled with the efforts of some to demean, persecute, and even eradicate Jews by expulsion or murder. These efforts have caused tragic rifts that have turned many Jews from considering Jesus of Nazareth to be the promised Messiah of the Jewish people.

• The blood of Jesus, when it is allowed to work to its fullness in the hearts of those who turn to him, eliminates the lesser differences between Jews and Gentiles and makes them—as Paul wrote to the Ephesians—"one new man."

5 A WORD ABOUT PROPHETIC UNDERSTANDING

ANY WHO READ THE BIBLE FAITHFULLY will confess to a hesitation when it comes to the prophetic sections of Scripture. The histories read like stories, the wisdom books feed our souls, and the doctrinal writings build our faith. But what are we to do with the prophecies? They're so *out there*, so distant and futuristic and hard to figure out. Things change, however, when we can see evidence of prophecies coming true in our time. Suddenly, these obtuse passages jump to life.

We are about to take a step forward in this book, moving from explanation and encouragement to an investigation of some of the prophecies of Scripture concerning Jews and Gentiles woven through Old Testament passages, confirmed in Paul's letter to the Romans, and unveiled with increasing clarity in our own time. We promise to do our best to keep this discussion close in to the Scriptures that support what we are seeing. And we believe that if you will explore these Scriptures with us, set against the evidence of God's move in the world today, you will be convinced in many if not all ways with us that this is a thrilling time to be a follower of Jesus Christ, with even more amazing times to come as God unfolds his plan on the earth.

PROGRESSIVE UNVEILING

Now we know this about Scripture's prophetic passages: they are made increasingly meaningful as time passes. This should not come as a surprise. If you were told by a friend that she was planning to take a trip abroad a year from now, you would notice increasing evidence of this fact as the year progressed—she saved her money, scheduled her flights, secured her passports and necessary visas, read travel guides, and eventually started packing her bags. The fruition of her plan would be "progressively unveiled" to you as she went through this series of activities.

Similarly, when God reveals his plans prophetically, those who hear them—even the prophets themselves!—ask themselves whether these plans can really be true, and maybe whether they are even possible. However, as time progresses and "the course of human events" begins to take shape, God's prophecies also take on a more definitive and supportable form. They don't become increasingly *true*, for they are the enduring words of God, the one who is absolutely faithful and true. However, these prophecies do become increasingly *evident*. This is particularly important because many prophecies, when they are first given, are nearly impossible to grasp. They either contain aspects that are not yet in place, or they may be interpreted in multiple ways.

In essence, we are now inviting you to see Scripture through a new interpretive grid, one that takes into account at least two major developments in our time: (1) the return of hundreds of thousands of Jews to the land of Israel and (2) the turning of Jewish hearts to Yeshua as the promised Messiah of God. This is no more radical an idea than to suggest that you do what the apostles did, for they saw the Old Testament with fresh eyes once Yeshua had been with them—old speculative meanings were replaced by new certain meanings. We encourage you to examine the Scriptures with us, much as the Bereans did, to see if what we teach is true. We think it is. But you are, of course, allowed to be your own judge.

We truly believe that the matters we are about to discuss, including insight into what may be coming in the seasons ahead, represent helpful explanations from the Lord, especially in light of what we see in the world around us today. But we also present them as humbly as we can, because we realize that many other committed and careful men and women of God have tried to make sense of this same material and have, at times, come to different conclusions. This does not mean that we think that they were wrong and we are right. Rather, it may mean that they have interpreted things according to the leading of God in their time and place, while we have been led to interpret them in our time and place. This may be the result of God's progressive unveiling, where we have the opportunity to see things in our time that others in the past could not.

Look at these important words of Jesus:

> "But blessed are your eyes because they see and your ears because they hear. For I tell you the truth, many prophets and righteous men longed to see what you see but did not see it, and to hear what you hear but did not hear it." (Matthew 13:16-17)

Jesus spoke these words in reference to the prophecies about himself—that his person and his work allowed people to perceive the prophecies openly, when even the most intent scholars could not make sense of them in the past. But many of the prophecies of both the Old and New Testaments were not pointed toward Jesus' first coming. Rather, they were pointed toward his second coming and the events that would precede, surround, and follow it—what theologians call "eschatology," or the study of the end times. Doesn't it make equal sense that the events and evidence of our time stand a good chance of helping us peel back the meaning of prophecies better than those in the past could do, especially if we truly are living in "the last days?"[21]

This means that we sometimes leave behind our partial understanding for a more complete understanding. It does not mean that we leap from current event to current event, constantly adjusting our perspective. In this book, we are writing of a "megatrend." The broader turning of Jewish hearts to Yeshua has now stretched past fifty years and continues to grow. It is a sustained move of God, but it has been largely unrecognized by the Gentile church. In our minds, a reassessment of some of the eschatological teaching that has existed for decades, and even centuries, is overdue.

But we are not the only ones currently engaged in this reassessment. Others in our present time may see things differently. Here we suggest that God, using the full spectrum of his church in Jesus Christ, unveils his purposes through the full council of believers, giving one piece of understanding to some and another piece of understanding to others. In the unity of Christ's body, we might bring these pieces of understanding together to increase our knowledge of God and his prophetically revealed plans. And by giving only a portion here and a portion there, God keeps each of us humble, but also charges us to share faithfully and boldly the piece he has given to us.

Thus, we do not make apologies for what we recognize according to what God has given us, except to acknowledge our human limitations. We love the spirit of a well-known pastor, who frequently asks the Lord to erase from his hearers' minds anything that he has taught that actually misses the heart or mind of God. We do the same here, asking for God's protective hand over what we will say in the chapters to follow, wanting him to carry forth only those things that are wholly true.

THE CHAPTER IN REVIEW

Prophetic Understanding

ONE BIG IDEA

The ability to understand prophecy as it is recorded in Scripture increases over time as the flow of earthly events makes components of these prophecies more recognizable.

KEY POINTS

• *Many people avoid reading the prophetic passages of Scripture because they seem ethereal or distant.*

• *As time passes, prophetic passages become increasingly meaningful as they are "progressively unveiled" through the unfolding of visible human activity, and as the Spirit-filled wisdom of God's gifted teachers converges.*

• *Ensuing discussions in this book will rely on what the authors see as evidence of current and coming fulfillment of biblical prophecy, freshly understood as they survey the world around us.*

• *Readers are encouraged to search the Scriptures for themselves, and to ask questions afresh—not because "new truth" is being presented here, but because enduring prophetic truth is becoming increasingly clear.*

6 SHEPHERDS AMONG THE PEOPLE

IN THE LAST CHAPTER OF THE OLD TESTAMENT book of Isaiah, the prophet delivers the LORD's words of hope for a coming day. This is a day when the enemies of God will be repaid "all they deserve," and the people of God will be returned to the land around Jerusalem.

Isaiah's prophecy was issued ahead of the exile of Judah, when the Jewish people were carted off by the Babylonians according to the judgment of God for their unfaithfulness to him. We know that after 70 years in captivity, a series of remarkably gracious allowances on the part of the rulers in Babylon made a way for the Jewish people to return to their land, where they rebuilt the walls and temple of Jerusalem. In many ways, this appeared to be the fulfillment of the prophecies of Isaiah.

But one aspect was out of whack. In verses 7 and 8 of that 66th chapter of Isaiah, God's words were these:

> "Before she goes into labor,
>   she gives birth;
> before the pains come upon her,
>   she delivers a son.
> Who has ever heard of such a thing?
>   Who has ever seen such things?

> Can a country be born in a day
>   or a nation be brought forth in a moment?
> Yet no sooner is Zion in labor
>   than she gives birth to her children."

When the Jewish people returned from Babylon, their "road to recovery" was a long one, including the defense of their families while they tried to rebuild the city and the temple. Yet Isaiah's prophecy had suggested a much swifter establishment of the Jewish nation than this. Those living in the time of the restoration of Israel under Ezra and Nehemiah, then, might have wondered about the difference between Isaiah's prophecy and the reality before them.

Most theologians no longer wonder. First, they know that the restored Israel of 400 BC lasted only until the Roman occupation in the century before Jesus, and then the destruction of the temple in 70 AD. Second, they are aware of the "one day" that was May 14, 1948. On this day, according to the declaration of the Jewish Agency, with the support of the United Nations, Israel was restored as a nation for the Jewish people, with borders in the ancient land on the eastern edge of the Mediterranean Sea. Within 24 hours, five Arab nations had declared war on Israel, but the international recognition of the Israeli state was in place—a country for God's people had been born in a day.

Of course, this begs an important question. In this book, we have identified *God's people* as those who agree together on salvation through the blood of Jesus. Certainly, this tenet is not accepted by the non-believing Jew.[22] Therefore, in this case, we are adhering to the definition of *God's people* at the time of Isaiah's prophecy, that is, those of Jewish descent. It was for these people specifically that Israel was made a nation in 1948.

However, let us also quickly remind ourselves that many thousand among the ethnic Jews are also now followers of Yeshua. And we believe that these people have an especially important role to play in the unfolding plan of God in Israel among nonbelieving Jews, as well as among Jews and Gentiles globally.

THE PROPHECIES AND FULFILLMENT OF *ALIYAH*

Throughout the Old Testament scriptures, you will find more than 700 references to the Jewish people making *aliyah,* or a return to their land. Consider passages like these:

> "But you, O mountains of Israel, will produce branches and fruit for my people Israel, for they will soon come home. I am concerned for you and will look on you with favor; you will be plowed and sown, and I will multiply the number of people upon you, even the whole house of Israel. The towns will be inhabited and the ruins rebuilt. I will increase the number of men and animals upon you, and they will be fruitful and become numerous. I will settle people on you as in the past and will make you prosper more than before. Then you will know that I am the LORD. I will cause people, my people Israel, to walk upon you. They will possess you, and you will be their inheritance; you will never again deprive them of their children." (Ezekiel 36:8-12)

> "Though I scatter them among the peoples,
>   yet in distant lands they will remember me.
> They and their children will survive,
>   and they will return.
> I will bring them back from Egypt
>   and gather them from Assyria.
> I will bring them to Gilead and Lebanon,

> and there will not be room enough for them."
> (Zechariah 10:9-10)

> "I myself will gather the remnant of my flock out of all
> the countries where I have driven them and will bring
> them back to their pasture, where they will be fruitful
> and increase in number. I will place shepherds over
> them who will tend them, and they will no longer be
> afraid or terrified, nor will any be missing," declares
> the LORD. (Jeremiah 23:3-4)

Scripturally, there is no doubt about God's intent to restore the people called Israel (the Jewish people) to the land called Israel. The prevalence of *aliyah* passages such as these makes this intention clear.

We must also turn our eyes to the historical developments of the past 130 years. Although small bands have through the centuries made *aliyah,* returning to Israel on their religious convictions, beginning in the 1880s increasingly larger groups of Jews have made organized returns to the land, settling there according to a variety of motivations—to flee persecution, to take advantage of political opportunities, and to dwell among fellow Jews. Regardless of the motivation, this series of returns has led to an ever-increasing population of Jewish people in Israel itself.[23] The Jewish Agency estimates that there are currently about 14 million Jewish people worldwide, with more than five million living in Israel.

These statistics mean little, of course, to a demographer whose job it is to report population figures and trends, except when they are compared to the existence of all people in all places. They mean a bit more, perhaps, to sociologists and anthropologists who try to dig into the known reasons people move from place to place. Certainly, the frequent persecution of the Jews in other parts of the world has driven many Jewish people to make *aliyah,* and this would be of particular interest to these social scientists. But when you are biblically interested and engaged in studying the prophecies of Scripture, the migration of more than three million Jews from places where they have built their homes and sometimes have enjoyed true freedom from persecution (like the United States) is of interest for an entirely different reason: it invites the question of whether God has begun to fulfill the prophecies of old about the return of the Jewish people to the land he chose for them. We believe the answer to that question is a resounding *yes.*

BELIEVING JEWS

Excitement over the return of the Jews to Israel may leave many Gentiles shaking their heads, wondering what all the fuss is about. In fact, when you consider the number of military actions that have resulted since 1948 between Israel and those opposed to the Israeli state, you may be tempted to question how a peace-minded follower of Christ can eagerly support the return of God's people to the land. And when many Jews remain opposed to the idea of Yeshua as the promised Messiah, the questions deepen.

In order to explain our own excitement, we need to back up to the fourth verse of Jeremiah 23, which we quoted above: "I will place shepherds over them who will tend them." We believe these shepherds are being established among the Jewish people in Israel; they are the Jewish believers, those who have affirmed Jesus as Messiah.

In the 1970s, two Jewish men began to speak and write openly about Yeshua as Messiah. The first of these was Moishe Rosen, the founder of Jews for Jesus in 1973. This group was blessed to make significant progress in articulating and advancing the Good News of Jesus among Jewish people. We love the fact that those active in Jews for Jesus, when asked how long Jews for Jesus has been around, like to answer, "Since 32 AD, give or take a year." These brothers and sisters in Yeshua are making the case that believing Jews have led the way for us all since Yeshua himself walked the earth. Sometimes, however, Jews for Jesus has been called into question by Jewish believers because the organization has been open to "assimilation"—that is, they have normally encouraged believing Jews to become connected with churches full of other believers, which in the United States (Jews for Jesus started in San Francisco) has predominantly meant Gentile congregations.

About the same time that Jews for Jesus was getting started, the Holy Spirit was moving in a man named Paul Liberman, a Jew who became a believer in Yeshua in 1971. Liberman, in his oft-reprinted book, *The Fig Tree Blossoms,* credits the Six-Day War between Israelis and Arabs in 1967 as the genesis of Messianic Jews, those who did not want their belief in Yeshua to separate them from their Jewish heritage. From that point forward, little by little, the number of individual Messianic Jews and Messianic Jewish congregations has grown steadily. Today it is estimated that more than a quarter million Jewish people profess faith in Yeshua. Of those, probably no more than 20,000 live in Israel. But may we say this: our hearts are with those 20,000!

In late 2009, our ministry (Links Players International) took a group of about 30 Gentile believers from the United States on a trip to Israel. The trip included some of the typical components of Holy Land expeditions, including visits to biblical sites and teaching that highlighted the contexts of the biblical accounts that were right in front of the travelers' eyes. But in addition to these visits, the American group had opportunity to interact several times with Messianic Jews living in Israel. These were not new contacts and friendships for us, but they were for the others on the trip. The experience was unforgettable. In one act of unity, some in the group pledged to raise $40,000 back home in the States in order to fund a playground for children who visited a Jewish retreat center operated by Messianic Jews. It was really a small gesture, and perhaps not exceedingly spiritual, but it sent a message to those believing Jews that their Gentile brothers and sisters heard the desires of their hearts for their children and were willing to stand with them in loving those children.

Why is this especially important? Perhaps the most visible reason Gentile believers need to stand with Jewish believers in Israel at this time is that those Jewish believers face persecution from some Orthodox factions, who accuse the Messianic Jews of leading Jews astray with their teachings about Yeshua. This is not new. In the same way, the apostle Paul and his colleagues were persecuted for suggesting that Yeshua, the carpenter from Nazareth, was the promised Messiah. The Jewish leaders of Paul's time felt that they were losing their grip on their people, and they fought strongly against the Way (the name given in the book of Acts to the movement of those who followed Jesus). Though Jesus was Jewish, his position as Messiah has never been received by mainstream Judaism, and contentions have arisen throughout history over this "stumbling block."

And yet we firmly believe that it is the Messianic Jews who are being raised up by God as the shepherds who will tend God's people. If we hold to the position that salvation does not come through the law but through faith—which is the difference between the Old Covenant and the New Covenant—then we must anticipate a New Covenant revival among non-believing Jews, in accordance with Ezekiel 36:24-28:

> "For I will take you out of the nations; I will gather
> you from all the countries and bring you back to your
> own land. I will sprinkle clean water on you, and you
> will be clean; I will cleanse you from all your impuri-
> ties and from all your idols. I will give you a new heart
> and put a new spirit in you; I will remove from you a
> heart of stone and give you a heart of flesh. And I
> will put my Spirit in you and move you to follow my
> decrees and be careful to keep my laws. You will live
> in the land I gave your forefathers; you will be my
> people, and I will be your God."

If you are a Gentile who has heard much teaching through the years in the local church, you have almost certainly heard this passage preached for its emphasis on the "heart of flesh" and "the Spirit in you." Look now, however, at the obvious focus of this passage not on Gentile believers but on the Jewish people—a return from the nations, a desire to follow God's voice[24], and residence in the land of the *Jewish* forefathers. Plainly, this is a New Covenant promise being made to the Old Covenant people. Their hearts will return to life, not by the law but by the Spirit of God. Faith will precede action in the hearts of the people God has always called his people. This is already happening among the minority of Jews known as Messianic believers! Does it not make full sense, then, that God will use these people as those most equipped and best positioned to reach non-believing Jews?

READY TO LEAD

We have grown careful in our Christian contexts about those

we allow to be leaders. There is biblical precedence for this, as Paul wrote to Timothy about the qualifications for elders—or leaders—in the early churches. So we understand that there is a need to be wise about declaring Messianic Jews the shepherds set to lead God's people into New Covenant faith.

What is exciting is that the prophetic passages of Scripture point to just such leaders, those who have been prepared and proven by God for the work at hand. God himself is qualifying those who will nurture, train and build the people of faith. The following paragraphs will give you confidence in God's Word and in those he is calling to lead.

First, these leaders have been *tested through persecution and judgment.* A thorough reading of the Old Testament shows that God often dispensed judgment on his people at the hands of their enemies. Persecution has come upon the Jews as God sought to temper them for his purposes. (Those who would dismiss a God who chooses some to bless and others to judge might take note of this fact! "Judgment," Scripture tells us, "begins with the family of God."[25]) Those who would lead the Jews into New Covenant relationship with God are no exception. Look:

"For this is what the Sovereign LORD says: How much worse will it be when I send against Jerusalem my four dreadful judgments—sword and famine and wild beasts and plague—to kill its men and their animals! Yet there will be some survivors—sons and daughters who will be brought out of it. They will come to you, and when you see their conduct and actions, you will be consoled regarding the disaster I have brought upon Jerusalem—every disaster I have brought upon it. You will be consoled when you see their conduct and their actions, for you will know that I have done nothing in

> it without cause, declares the Sovereign LORD." (Ezekiel
> 14:21-23)

God has made a habit, each time that his people have generally
wandered away from him, of maintaining a "remnant" of faithful men and women. It is these righteous people that he uses
to reestablish his people. If, as we know from Paul's writing to
the Romans, New Covenant righteousness is the righteousness
that comes from faith, then this remnant among Jews today
must be those living by faith in Yeshua.

Second, these leaders will *care for the people of God* in a way
that they have not been cared for in the past. The opening verses of Ezekiel 34 reveal a distraught God, for those who had
been established in the past as the shepherds of his people had
neglected the sheep. They had been left to their own wander-
ings and now were scattered over the earth. As we continue
through this rich chapter, we find that God will bring "David" to shepherd his people. At the time of Ezekiel's prophecy, however, David himself had been dead for more than 300
years. This David of whom God spoke was the one born in the
line of David—the Messiah, Yeshua. He would shepherd God's
people, tending to them as "prince among them."

Two passages in Jeremiah serve to support the Ezekiel 34
passage, as they refer to new shepherds who will be brought to
care for the flock of God:

> "Return, faithless people," declares the LORD, "for I am
> your husband. I will choose you—one from a town and
> two from a clan—and bring you to Zion. Then I will
> give you shepherds after my own heart, who will lead
> you with knowledge and understanding." (Jeremiah
> 3:14-15)

> "I myself will gather the remnant of my flock out of all
> the countries where I have driven them and will bring
> them back to their pasture, where they will be fruitful
> and increase in number. I will place shepherds over
> them who will tend them, and they will no longer be
> afraid or terrified, nor will any be missing," declares
> the LORD. (Jeremiah 23:3-4)

How can this be? How can one passage suggest that the Messiah alone will shepherd the sheep, while these other passages point to a number of shepherds? The common answer to this question makes common sense: those noted as pastors (shepherds) in the New Covenant church have never seen themselves as the Good Shepherd, Jesus, but as undershepherds. And those who have been blessed to mature spiritually under the care of an excellent pastor know that these undershepherds display the heart of the Good Shepherd in the work they do among his people. Again, we see that Messianic Jews will be equipped with such a Messiah-heart to give away in shepherd's service to their Jewish friends.

Third, these leaders will *walk in humility and truth*. This should come as no surprise; these are traits we all desire in our Jesus-honoring leaders. In a prophetic passage that the New International Version titles "The Future of Jerusalem," we read of these very traits:

> "On that day you will not be put to shame
>   for all the wrongs you have done to me,
> because I will remove from this city
>   those who rejoice in their pride.
> Never again will you be haughty
>   on my holy hill.
> But I will leave within you

> the meek and humble,
>   who trust in the name of the LORD.
> The remnant of Israel will do no wrong;
>   they will speak no lies,
>   nor will deceit be found in their mouths.
> They will eat and lie down
>   and no one will make them afraid."
> (Zephaniah 3:11-13)

Thus, humility and truth are definitive marks of the remnant God has kept for himself, those who will lead his chosen people from the law to faith.

Fourth, these leaders will *demonstrate the abiding presence of God.* What perfect sense this makes if this is to be the final return of God's people to their place in him! When God is close to the heart of a person, it is evident in the outworking of that person's life. We see in them joy and forthrightness, a willingness to serve and openly talk about the work of God. Not only does a life like this point the way for Jews, but for Gentiles as well:

> This is what the LORD Almighty says: "In those days ten men from all languages will take hold of one Jew by the hem of his robe and say, 'Let us go with you, because we have heard that God is with you.'" (Zechariah 8:23)

> This is what the LORD says:
> "The products of Egypt and the merchandise of
>   Cush,
>   and those tall Sabeans—
> they will come over to you
>   and will be yours;
> they will trudge behind you,

> coming over to you in chains.
> They will bow down before you
>   and plead with you saying,
> 'Surely God is with you, and there is no other;
>   there is no other God.'" (Isaiah 45:14)

Nearly every believer we have ever encountered has expressed the hope that non-believers would look at their life and "see a difference." They would notice the light that is shining with us (and not hiding under a bushel), and they would desire to possess the assurance of salvation and nearness with God that we possess.

It is important to note here before moving on, however, two other important aspects of these passages. First, unlike some prophetic passages, which may have been fulfilled in one way but may also await a second fulfillment[26], we have no indication that the Jewish people have ever experienced this kind of appreciation from non-Jews—quite the opposite. Therefore, these passages await a first fulfillment. Also, we must note that these passages point specifically to Jews who will do this work. "Replacement theology" often suggests that the Jewish people have been replaced by the entire body of believers, including Gentiles, and that the Old Testament prophecies once meant for the Jews alone may now be applied to all believers. But these passages (as well as the passages in Romans 11 that we will explore in the next chapter) maintain a separation of the prophetic for those who are Jewish and those who may be called "spiritual Israel" (all believers).

Fifth, the rising leaders are *equipped as true priests and ministers.* This equipping will include the ability to unite and rebuild the people after generations of failure. We find remarkable evidence of this in the prophecies of Isaiah, immediately following the Yeshua-pointing passage about the Messiah, operating with the Spirit's covering, preaching good news to the poor and proclaiming freedom for the captives:

> [Those set free by the Messiah] will rebuild the
>   ancient ruins
>   and restore the places long devastated;
> they will renew the ruined cities
>   that have been devastated for generations.
> Aliens will shepherd your flocks;
>   foreigners will work your fields and vineyards.
> And you will be called priests of the LORD,
>   you will be named ministers of our God.
> You will feed on the wealth of nations,
>   and in their riches you will boast. (Isaiah 61:4-6)

Again we see a Jewish leadership, for foreigners will dwell among them as workers of the livestock and the land, but those called "priests and ministers" are those who belong to the land. As we will discuss in chapter 8, there is much to be done together between believing Jew and believing Gentile, but here the prophet points to something of a role difference that we would recognize in earthly terms, with the Jewish believers taking the lead.

WILLING TO BE LED

We hope that you can understand our excitement about this kind of leader among the Jewish people. In fact, we are excited ourselves to be led by such people—those whose hearts are attuned to God's voice and whose minds are affixed to his Word. More than that, the heritage of these leaders equips them with an understanding of the types and shadows of the Old Testament writings that point to the Spirit-filled fulfillment of those passages in the life of Christ, the life of the apostles, and our own lives! Yeshua was Jewish; it makes perfect sense then that the "light to the Gentiles"[27] will be Jewish men and women who believe in him as Messiah.

But questions remain. Chiefly, what will it take for Jews to turn in greater numbers to Jesus? As we noted in chapter 4, Paul wrote to the Romans that "because of [the Jews'] transgressions, salvation has come to the Gentiles to make Israel envious" (Romans 8:11). Envy often will turn our eyes, but it will rarely turn our hearts. What does turn our hearts is the kindness of God (Romans 2:4), often displayed in the reflected kindness of those who believe in him. No one is in a better position to show this kindness—and to bring the Good News of Yeshua—amidst non-believing Jews than Jews who have already come to the Messiah and experienced the wonder of Yeshua in their hearts and in their lives.

It is by wonder upon wonder that revivals happen. It is by wonder upon wonder that "all Israel will be saved." To this grand possibility we turn our eyes in the next chapter.

THE CHAPTER IN REVIEW

Shepherds among God's People

ONE BIG IDEA

God will raise up new shepherds among his beloved people, to instruct and admonish them according to the word and heart of the Lord. These shepherds will come from the growing band of Jewish believers.

KEY POINTS

• The land of Israel has been reestablished primarily for the people of Israel (Jews). Since 1948, Jewish people have been making aliyah, returning to the land.

• Among those returning are Messianic Jews, or Jews who believe that Yeshua is the promised Messiah. There are roughly 20,000 such believing Jews in Israel today.

• God has prepared the hearts of these believing Jews through persecution and judgment. This chastening has produced a deep caring for their own people. As leaders they will walk in humility and truth and demonstrate the abiding presence of God.

• Those Gentiles who see this kind of leadership among believing Jews must prepare to support and encourage such leaders in their ministry—including being led by them!

7 'PENTECOST 2'

FIFTY DAYS AFTER THE JEWISH CELEBRATION OF the Passover, the Jewish religious community holds another feast, this one, Shavuot, commemorating the giving of the Torah (the Law) at Mount Sinai. In the year of Jesus' death, this same feast was more commonly known among the Hellenistic Jews as Pentecost, meaning "fiftieth day," because of its chronological relationship to Passover. Thus, the second chapter of Acts begins with these words: "When the day of Pentecost came…"

The Christian tradition down through the centuries has carried forth that name, Pentecost, as a celebration of what happened that day in Jerusalem——the coming of the Holy Spirit upon the gathered believers in Yeshua.

Because Peter knew the Scriptures and was assured that "the Sovereign LORD does nothing without revealing his plans to his servants the prophets,"[28] it likely came as no surprise to him that what he was witnessing among his fellow believers that day——the violent wind, the tongues of fire, and the unknown languages spoken spontaneously——was being confirmed in his own spirit as a fulfillment of the words of the prophet Joel. And so he began to preach that: "[What you are seeing and hearing] is what was spoken by the prophet Joel: 'In the last days, God says, I will pour out my Spirit on all people.'"

Here was the first indication in the apostles' teaching that the Messiah's work had been rendered for all, both Jews and Gentiles, though it would be some time yet before the Spirit came upon the Gentile home of Cornelius. More significant on this day of Pentecost was that Jesus' own Messianic position and authority were being confirmed and preached in the open. Jews on the whole were being given the opportunity to place their faith in Yeshua, just as the gathered disciples had already done. And on the whole, the words of Peter were regarded with great interest. On that day alone, three thousand Jews "were added to their number"—a 25-fold increase in the number of believers. In the ensuing weeks and months, we know, "the Lord added to their number daily those who were being saved."

Belief was not universal among the Jews of the time, of course, and those in positions of Jewish leadership and power were especially resistant. Persecution of the believers came from both the Roman political leaders and the Jewish religious establishment, in that the worship of Yeshua presented a challenge to the emperor of Rome (deemed to be the preeminent God) and the "God is One" Shema of the Jews.

It is with this historical understanding in mind that we return to Paul's letter to the Romans, particularly eyeing the closing passages of chapter 11.

THE CHOICE ALL PEOPLE MUST MAKE

The choice that confronted each Jew in Jerusalem on that ancient day of Pentecost is the same choice that confronts all Jewish people today: are they prepared to apply the Old Testament prophecies about the Jewish Messiah to this man Yeshua of Nazareth? If you are a believer yourself, it is tempting to think, *The choice is obvious. The evidence is right there in front of you*. But it was not an obvious choice that Pentecost day. Some believed, yes. But many others did not. Likewise, on the day that Jesus raised Lazarus from the dead, we read that "many of the Jews…put their faith in him," but also that "some of them went to the Pharisees and told them what Jesus had done"— that is, they gave the religious leaders fuel for their anti-Jesus fire.

Thus, we must confirm that the Holy Spirit, who is the Spirit of Christ, must move in the heart of a person if he or she is to believe. The choice can be laid open, but the decision cannot be forced, not even by the most eloquent apologist or the most adamant preacher. Revival comes not at the hands, voices or even wills of men; it comes only by the power of the Spirit of God.

For this reason, we are so pleased to see the work of God among Jewish people in our own time as they come face to face with Yeshua and declare him the Messiah and Lord of their lives. We delight in each one that is saved, rejoicing with the angels in heaven! But we are also aware that Messianic Jews still represent only a very small portion of all Jews everywhere. And until believing Jews and non-believing Jews have opportunity to sit together and converse about this most important matter, the choice is not being laid open for most Jewish people. So, we are thrilled when both mainstream Jews and Messianic Jews make *aliyah*, returning to Israel to live, for it is in this context that they are likeliest to meet and talk. It is in this context that the Good News of Yeshua can be passed from one Jew to another. And it is in this context that the Spirit of God will move upon the ancient chosen people of God, bringing them back into life with him. Look:

And if they (the Jews) do not persist in unbelief, they will

> be grafted in, for God is able to graft them in again. After all, if you (Gentiles) were cut off of an olive tree that is wild by nature, and contrary to nature were grafted into a cultivated olive tree, how much more readily will these, the natural branches, be grafted into their own olive tree! (Romans 11:23-24, parenthetical insertions added)

The way is open for any Jewish man or woman to make a decision for Jesus based in faith and be included among the people who are chosen not by race or by cosmetic action (circumcision) but by faith in the only one who can save them, Yeshua. We believe that this very thing will happen among a great number of Jews in a sort of "Pentecost 2."

Why do we dare to think such a thing?

We must begin by understanding that many Jews have for centuries been veiled from a full understanding of Jesus, as allowed by God:

> I do not want you, brethren, to be uninformed of this mystery—so that you will not be wise in your own estimation—that a partial hardening has happened to Israel until the fullness of the Gentiles has come in. (Romans 11:25, NASB)

These words contain an explicit explanation and an implicit prophecy. First, we are told that God's chief thrust for a long period of time until now has been to save Gentiles through the Messiah. This has been matched, in God's sovereign plan, by a reluctance on the part of most Jews to believe that Jesus could be this Messiah. Instead, they have believed that the Messiah is yet to come—or, as many secular Jews have done, they have dismissed the notion of a Messiah (and perhaps God himself) altogether. However, the day is coming when "the fullness of the Gentiles" will have come in. Up to our present age, the primary thrust of God's saving work through Jesus has been to the Gentiles. But as we can infer from this amazing passage, the day is coming when the door will be thrown wide open again to the Jewish people. And this is why we read in the next verse of Romans 11: "All Israel will be saved."

There are questions, of course, about the full parameters of "all Israel," and we will address those shortly, but for the moment let's review the picture we have been given:

- First, Jewish people from all parts of the world will increasingly make *aliyah*, returning to the physical land of Israel. Some of these Jews will be believers in Yeshua as Messiah, but the vast majority will not.

- Next, Messianic Jews will be uniquely prepared and positioned by God to carry the truth about Yeshua into the land and among non-believing Jews. They will be the preeminent witnesses to the Good News of Yeshua among their own people.

- Finally, after "the fullness of the Gentiles" has come to belief in Jesus, a massive outpouring of the Gospel, with eyes and ears of faith opened powerfully by the Holy Spirit, will occur among the Jewish people in Israel. We dare to call this "Pentecost 2," but we really make no specific suggestions about what this will look like or how swiftly it will occur.

It is very important, however, that we not lay out these ideas without continuing the prophetic support of the Scriptures that we have shown you elsewhere, for we see great evidence in the prophecies for such a revival, if we can call it that, among God's historically chosen people.

JEWISH REVIVAL PROPHECIES

We are fully aware that the term "revival" does not occur in the actual text of Scripture (though it is sometimes used to describe sections of the Bible in the inserted subheadings of translators). In fact, we wonder if the term isn't often misapplied when it is used to mean a refreshing or renewal of believers. But in this case, when we are referring to a people that has been written off as dead in numerous ways—genetically by fascists, geographically by historians, spiritually by opposing religious leaders—we find the word to be most appropriate. In the times ahead, be they very near or somewhat farther out, we are persuaded that revival will happen for the Jewish people. Let's investigate some passages that have served to convince us.

> Then the LORD will be jealous for his land
>   and take pity on his people.
> The LORD will reply to them:
> "I am sending you grain, new wine and oil,
>   enough to satisfy you fully;
> never again will I make you
>   an object of scorn to the nations." (Joel 2:18)

And further down in this passage:

> "You will have plenty to eat, until you are full,
>   and you will praise the name of the LORD your God,
>   who has worked wonders for you;
> never again will my people be shamed.

Then you will know that I am in Israel,
> that I am the LORD your God,
> and that there is no other;
never again will my people be shamed." (Joel 2:26-27)

Among the wonderful promises of these verses and the several that surround them——including the pointing to the land of Israel——is this key phrase: "never again." These are the words that specifically identify these prophecies with the Jewish people, who have repeatedly been shamed throughout history and in many lands. They are also the words that identify a "last work" of God among the Jews, and indicate finality to his earthly plans ahead of the establishment of a new heaven and a new earth under the rule of Christ.

But more amazing still is that this passage is followed immediately by the passage Peter preached on at "Pentecost 1."

"And afterward,
> I will pour out my Spirit on all people.
Your sons and daughters will prophesy,
> your old men will dream dreams,
> your young men will see visions.
Even on my servants, both men and women,
> I will pour out my Spirit in those days.
I will show wonders in the heavens
> and on the earth,
> blood and fire and billows of smoke.
The sun will be turned to darkness
> and the moon to blood
> before the coming of the great and dreadful day of
> > the LORD.
And everyone who calls
> on the name of the LORD will be saved;
for on Mount Zion and in Jerusalem

> there will be deliverance,
>   as the LORD has said,
> among the survivors
>   whom the LORD calls." (Joel 2:28-32)

Again we find key phrases that inform our understanding. First, we recognize that this outpouring comes "afterward," that is, after the Jews return to their land and are established in prosperity. Second, we see that this will indeed be a work of the Holy Spirit. Third, we see by the inclusion of sons and daughters, old and young, and male and female servants that this will be a widespread revival, reaching all echelons of Jewish society. Fourth, we find that this will be an obvious work of God accompanied by signs and wonders ahead of his eternal plans. And fifth, we notice that this is a work that will happen in the land of Israel, where we find Mount Zion and Jerusalem. We also find that this will be a work "among the survivors whom the LORD calls," which helps us understand the meaning of "all Israel," but again we will wait to work through that matter.[29] Moreover, we understand this to be a dually fulfilled passage, as seen once at Pentecost in Acts 2, and in the time to come when "never again will my people be shamed." What a glorious day that will be for all believing Jewish people and for all other believers who stand with them!

Revival, of course, is nearly always marked by a godly sorrow among the people. The Spirit brings people to a place of repentance, wherein they are willing to exchange their "business as usual" for true righteousness before the LORD. Consider these essential passages from the prophecies of Ezekiel:

> "Then in the nations where they have been carried captive, those who escape will remember me—how I have been grieved by their adulterous hearts, which

have turned away from me, and by their eyes, which have lusted after idols. They will loathe themselves for the evil they have done and for all their detestable practices." (Ezekiel 6:9)

"I will accept you as fragrant incense when I bring you out from the nations and gather you from the countries where you have been scattered, and I will show myself holy among you in the sight of the nations. Then you will know that I am the LORD, when I bring you into the land of Israel, the land I had sworn with uplifted hand to give to your fathers. There you will remember your conduct and all the actions by which you have defiled yourselves, and will loathe yourselves for the evil you have done. You will know that I am the LORD, when I deal with you for my name's sake and not according to your evil ways and your corrupt practices, O house of Israel, declares the Sovereign LORD." (Ezekiel 20:41-44)

It is plain here that God's people, those who would return to him in righteousness, will divorce themselves from the way they have previously lived their lives—without faith in him. The heart stirrings of this repentance may begin wherever Jews reside, but many will not repent until they have returned to Israel itself. There they will "remember [their] conduct" and return to the Lord. From this humble position, God will lift up his people, restoring them to himself for his name's sake. [30]

Of course, this kind of repentance often comes from both a Spirit-led awareness of one's sin and an eye-opening encounter with the revealed word of God. In the time of Hezekiah, king of Judah, as well as the time of Ezra's priestly leadership upon the return of the Babylonian captives, the reading of the Law of God, with a fresh anointing from the LORD for hearing and receiving the truth of His word, produced national revival among the Jewish people. Do we see the same dynamic recurring in the coming fulfillment of this prophecy of Isaiah?

> Is it not yet a little while
> > Before Lebanon will be turned into a fertile field
> > And the fertile field will be considered as a
> > > forest?
> On that day the deaf will hear words of a book,
> > And out of the gloom and the darkness the eyes of
> > > the blind will see. (Isaiah 29:17-18, NASB)

The current replanting and restoration of the forests of Israel and Lebanon lead us to believe that the time indicated by Isaiah may now be approaching rapidly. We are thrilled at the possibility of seeing so many people freshly "hear the words" and "see" what God is offering through Yeshua.

Apart from the work of the Spirit in the ears, eyes and hearts of the people, however, there will be other signs of revival as well. The first of these is the establishment of "the mountain of the LORD" on the earth. Here is an exciting prophetic vision of this event:

> In the last days
> the mountain of the LORD's temple will be established
> > as chief among the mountains;
> it will be raised above the hills,
> > and all the nations will stream to it.
> > Many peoples will come and say,
> > > "Come, let us go up to the mountain of the LORD,
> > > to the house of the God of Jacob.
> He will teach us his ways,
> > so that we may walk in his paths."

The law will go out from Zion,
　　the word of the LORD from Jerusalem.
He will judge between the nations
　　and will settle disputes for many peoples.
They will beat their swords into plowshares
　　and their spears into pruning hooks.
Nation will not take up sword against nation,
　　nor will they train for war anymore.
Come, O house of Jacob,
　　let us walk in the light of the LORD. (Isaiah 2:2-5)

What a wonder this prophecy is (as is its mirrored passage in Micah 4:1-8)! It speaks of an actual physical location—the mountain of the LORD—from which his peace will go out. While it is tempting to read this passage as a Zionist (one who is zealous for the sovereignty of the nation of Israel), it is more joyous to read it as one who is zealous instead for the sovereignty of God. The world frequently cries for peace, even appealing to this biblical passage, forgetting that the peace will come from One LORD through one people to many. That One LORD is the God of Abraham, Isaac, and Jacob, and that one people is the house of Jacob, the Jewish people.

Where will this mountain be? The passage makes it clear that the mountain will be in Jerusalem. It is from this ancient home to the Jewish people that God will cause great revival among his people, reaching from them to the nations. This is happening now! Europeans and Africans are standing together as brothers and sisters in Jesus, praying at the ancient sites in and around Jerusalem. People of all backgrounds are looking to Israel to learn God's ways, in accordance with Jeremiah 12:16:

"And if they learn well the ways of my people and

swear by my name, saying, 'As surely as the LORD lives'—even as they once taught my people to swear by Baal—then they will be established among my people."

Consider another prophecy that defines the scope of this work, one that immediately follows God's promise to establish "shepherds after my own heart" among the Jewish people:

"In those days, when your numbers have increased greatly in the land," declares the LORD, "men will no longer say, 'The ark of the covenant of the LORD.' It will never enter their minds or be remembered; it will not be missed, nor will another one be made. At that time they will call Jerusalem The Throne of the LORD, and all nations will gather in Jerusalem to honor the name of the LORD. No longer will they follow the stubbornness of their evil hearts." (Jeremiah 3:16-17)

We might note here that the ark of the covenant, famed as it may be, is only an instrument of religious expression. There was no life in the ark itself. Those who desire the restoration of such objects in the place of a revival of hearts through God himself are missing the true glory of God's greatest work. But those who recognize him for who he is—the Lord of salvation—realize quickly that all of the religious pieces are unnecessary. They were objects of the Old Covenant, while the New Covenant is marked by Immanuel, God with us. What will emanate from Jerusalem will not be an old religion, but rather the Ancient of Days. And because it will be God himself who reigns from The Throne of the LORD, his work will be undeniable and the believing will come from all nations to honor him.

Confirmation of this internal, spiritual work of God in the hearts of people—as opposed to widespread restoration of religious practices—arises from the New Covenant-pointing prophecies of Jeremiah and Ezekiel:

> "This is the covenant I will make with the house of
>   Israel
>   after that time," declares the Lord.
> "I will put my law in their minds
>   and write it on their hearts.
> I will be their God, and they will be my people.
> No longer will a man teach his neighbor, or a man his
> brother, saying, 'Know the Lord' because they will all
> know me, from the least of them to the greatest," declares
> the Lord. For I will forgive their wickedness and remember
> their sins no more." (Jeremiah 31:33-34)

> "When I have brought them (the Jews) back from the
> nations and have gathered them from the countries of
> their enemies, I will show myself holy through them in
> the sight of many nations. Then they will know that I
> am the Lord their God, for though I sent them into exile
> among the nations, I will gather them to their own land,
> not leaving any behind. I will no longer hide my face
> from them, for I will pour out my Spirit on the house of
> Israel, declares the Sovereign Lord." (Ezekiel 39:27-
> 29)

In both of these passages, we see a meeting between the natural return of the Jewish people to Israel and the supernatural return of the people to Yahweh. Though the thought is intolerable now to nearly all non-believing Jews, those of us—Jews and Gentiles both—who carry the great hope of salvation in Jesus the Messiah know that this revival will come as the work of the Spirit of Jesus—that is, through the Holy Spirit pointing men, women and children to Jesus, the risen Redeemer. Only by the Spirit is such a revival possible.

WHAT OF 'ALL ISRAEL'?

We cannot move past this point without wrestling, as promised, with the phrasing from Romans 11, verse 26: "And so all Israel will be saved…"

It does not seem possible, in light of what we know from other Scriptures, including Paul's own letter here, that "all Israel" could mean *all* Israel, with every last Jewish person being saved. Even non-believing Jews, who would otherwise love to seize on this passage as an immutable promise, are left to wonder about those who have married Gentile spouses—are their children to be counted as part of *all* Israel? And certainly, our theological discussions run amok when we try to spiritualize Israel to, in every case, mean "those who believe."

So what are we to do when the same Paul who wrote "my heart's desire and prayer to God for the Israelites is that they may be saved" (Romans 10:1) sweepingly declares "all Israel will be saved"?

Only this: that those dwelling in Israel at the time of this "second Pentecost" will be saved. Not because of their presence there. But because their hearts will be turned to the Messiah. As Paul explained, the Jewish people are loved by God—a love that is irrevocable. So it is by God's mercy that those who have lived with a disobedient lack of faith will be returned to the fold, saved by the Shepherd, and nurtured by the undershepherds whose faith in Yeshua has been cultivated in anticipation of this day.

That is our impression, but it is also held up by a close examination of the text itself. Romans 11:25 certainly refers to the Jewish people when it says, "Israel has experienced a hardening in part until the full number of the Gentiles has come in." For this reason, we would set a trap for ourselves by declaring that the very next verse——the "all Israel" verse——points not to physical Jews but to a spiritual collection of already saved Jews and Gentiles. Moreover, the continuation of verse 26 draws from Isaiah's prophecies in quoting "he will turn godlessness away from Jacob." The Jacob reference adds a specifically Jewish bull's eye to the target of Paul's words. We also recognize additional references to the broadly delivered salvation of the Jews in Romans 11:12 ("...how much greater riches will [the Jews'] fullness bring!") and Romans 11:15 ("...what will their acceptance be but life from the dead?").[31]

Can we say that this will include every last living Jewish person in Israel? We are not sure, but we anticipate the massive revival of which we have been speaking would set up the possibility of all or nearly all Israel being saved by God's mercy "on them all."

Can we say that this applies to Jews who have died in unbelief? Almost certainly not. If this were true, there would have been no point to Paul's prayer "for the Israelites that they may be saved." Neither would he have made it clear that "not all the Israelites accepted the good news" (Romans 10:16). But Paul also wrote, with a notable strength to his words: "For there is no difference between Jew and Gentile——the same Lord is the Lord of all and richly blesses all who call on him, for, 'Everyone who calls on the name of the Lord will be saved'" (Romans 10:12-13). What is critical is that this is not the same "LORD" translated *Yahweh* (the God of Abraham, Isaac and Jacob) in the Old Testament, but rather "Lord"——a ruling man, who is Jesus Christ, something we know from Romans 10:9: "...if you confess with your mouth, 'Jesus is Lord,' and believe in your heart that God raised him from the dead, you will be saved." How can this possibly happen among a people who for centuries have been opposed to the proclamation that Jesus of Nazareth was and is the promised Messiah of Israel? Only by a Spirit-charged revival. Only by a "Pentecost 2."

A COUPLE OF QUALIFIERS BEFORE WE CONTINUE

As we close this chapter, we are aware that some readers may be caught on a couple of sticking points.

The first of these is that some of the prophetic passages to which we have pointed in order to suggest a coming Jewish revival in Christ may not be absolutely recognizable as applying to this context. We realize this. We also know it was true of many of the prophetic passages to which the New Testament writers referred. Until God unveils the context of a particular prophetic passage to a teacher, it often remains clouded from our understanding. It is of critical importance to us that we do not try to stretch any Scripture beyond its obvious meaning; and as we noted in chapter 5, if we are seeing certain Scriptures mistakenly, we ask that God would dismiss any lasting impact of what we have said about them. Still, we believe that what we have laid before you is "of the Lord" and faithful to his word. We trust that he will align your spirit with us if we are truly delivering what he would have you hear.

We also know that some of you—particularly those well-versed in at least one framework of eschatology (the study of the end times)—may recognize aspects of what we have written as contrary to the studies you have done. We hope most importantly that this in no way diminishes what we have said in earlier chapters, especially as we have tried to convey our hearts for the salvation of the Jewish people by their Messiah, whom we believe to be Yeshua of Nazareth. We know that

Scripture tells us that our salvation as Gentiles comes by way of the Jews and thus compels us to honor and love them with the love of Jesus. This is our most important message, and why we have threaded it throughout this book. But we hope, too, that in our final chapter, where we explore some of the implications of this book on various eschatological or millennial views, you will recognize our appreciation for what you already believe, and for the millennial views of others, as well as understand some fresh insight that may be emerging for all eschatological camps in light of what is happening in the world around us today——that is, as we witness the progressive unveiling of God's ancient prophecies in our own time.

THE CHAPTER IN REVIEW

'Pentecost 2'

ONE BIG IDEA

Just as the initial coming of the Holy Spirit in Jerusalem ignited a large turning of Jewish hearts to God through Yeshua, we anticipate a 'second Pentecost' of broad spiritual revival among the Jewish people.

KEY POINTS

• While the personal choice for salvation is evident—go with Jesus or not—the Holy Spirit must move in the heart of each person, inspiring the faith to believe.

• A significant volume of biblical prophecy points to a widescale revival among the Jewish people. The word revival is certainly fitting for the Jews, as they have often been consigned to death, either literally by evil despots or figuratively by theological argumentation.

• The essence of revival among Jews is contained in the understanding that Jesus is Immanuel, God with us. Direct relationship with him trumps religious tradition of all kinds and establishes salvation for each one who believes.

• Paul's phrasing, "all Israel," indeed points toward a massive revival among Jewish people.

8 GLOBAL IMPACT OF JEWISH RESTORATION

A S YOU HAVE LIKELY GATHERED BY NOW, while our eyes are enamored with Israel, they are not fixed there. If the Jewish people are destined by God to be "a light to the nations" and widespread restoration comes to them through Jesus, the impact will be much greater than the boundaries of any nation can contain. In other words, by asking you to allow the words of the ancient prophets to come to life in your mind, we are asking you to envision a time of profound and substantive global change. And yet, we are certain that this age of change has already begun! Modern day Peters and Johns are emerging even now. We cannot ignore them.

Without question, the early Jewish remnant of believers in Jesus spread a gospel that could not be contained—its impact reached to the ends of the earth, just as Jesus had directed and foreseen. Knowing that these early believers form part of the "great cloud of witnesses" to the work of God among us, we've often wondered if they sit back in awe at the course of the last 2000 years. Imagine the untold joy they must experience having witnessed the emergence of true followers of Jesus in virtually every corner of the earth! The world has forever been changed by the words and actions of Jesus. And it was the hands and feet of the believing Jewish disciples that were sacrificially given over to the Messiah for his purposes of global reconciliation——they submitted themselves to him and became the conduit of the kingdom of God on earth.

Though the impact of the apostolic age has not ceased, we are strongly convinced that there is, even now, a renewed and growing emergence of "fresh impact" that will be felt across the planet. Small pictures are already being seen today.

In 2010, in Nazareth, Arab followers of Jesus invited Jewish followers of Jesus to join them in a day of prayer. During this time, worship was conducted by Jewish and Arab believers alike. They danced together, prayed together and in an act of supreme humility, the Arab believers began to wash the feet of the Jewish believers. They joined in prayer for Israel and the advancement of the kingdom. This is not a scene that was covered by any news agency, but it was a picture long ago foreseen by the prophets.

MIDDLE EAST PEACE?

Daily we hear about governmental attempts to fashion a "new" peace in the Middle East. There are always talks, talks and more talks——none of which seem to ease the tensions or secure any lasting results. Like it or not, this constant unrest has real implications for the global economy and global peace in general. What's the answer? Given the track record of the diplomatic strivings, the Nazareth prayer meeting may offer us a clue. Life in the Messiah is the answer to the question of peace in the Middle East! Consider what was revealed to the ancient Jewish prophets hundreds of years ago.

Isaiah saw:

- A day where there would be a highway from Egypt

to Assyria (modern day Iraq), where the two peoples would worship together along with a third party—Israel, described as a blessing in the midst of the earth. (Isaiah 19:18-25)

- A day where Arab nations will bring their wealth to Israel and worship alongside the Jewish people. This is happening today in small but perceptible ways. (Isaiah 60)

Jeremiah saw:

- A day when the nations would admit that their fathers' gods and religious strivings were worthless and unprofitable. This would occur in the context of the Jewish people regaining their land and returning to Israel.

Zechariah saw:

- A day when the Philistines (the modern Gaza Strip) would put aside their detestable practices and become a remnant for the God of Abraham, Isaac and Jacob. (Zechariah 9:6, 7)

This is just a sampling of the great hope the prophets give us for the reign of the Messiah. Of course, many people place some of these events much later, after Jesus has come back and set up his government in Jerusalem during a future millennial reign. However, as we witness a progressive unveiling of the plans God has had from the beginning for the restoration of all things (Acts 3:21), we allow for the opening of hearts to Yeshua all over the Middle East. How discouraging to men and women who feel they have heard the voice of the Creator calling them as missionaries to these hostile lands to be told that the revival God has caused them to desire will never happen because "our theology of the end times" won't allow for it!

Spiritual regeneration in Jesus is happening *today* among Jews, Arabs, and Gentiles of all kinds in lands once closed politically and spiritually. Observer and author Joel Rosenberg chooses as some of his favorite accounts the dreams and visions from God that have led formerly acrimonious people—including many Muslims—into relationship with Jesus. In this way, God has often been his own witness among Arab individuals and communities.

However, God is at the same time raising up believers who will venture into these territories for the sake of Christ. Here they will be able, like Philip, to answer the honest questions of those who have searched Scripture or encountered God through a miracle or vision and aren't sure what step to take next. Because this will be a ministry in the Middle East first, we have every reason to believe that Jewish believers will form this missionary band. And why not? For God is simultaneously raising questions in the hearts of Arabs and raising up believing leaders from among the Jewish people.

'AS GOES ISRAEL, SO GO THE NATIONS'

It is an old saying: "As goes Israel, so go the nations." And in the West, this notion has been guarded among politicos, Zionists, and religious friends of Israel alike. In the summer of 2010, former Spanish Prime Minister José María Aznar wrote a piece for the *London Times* in which he flatly stated, "If Israel goes down, we all go down."[32] By now, you should recognize that our own interests are not political (though we do pay attention to political developments in Israel and the surrounding nations). We are instead interested in the spiritual impact the believing people of Israel will have on the world.

It has long been a conviction among many Messianic Jews that the eleventh chapter of Romans provides us with a sort of hidden key to the Jewish impact for the kingdom of Jesus on the nations.

> Again I ask: Did [the Jewish people] stumble so as to fall beyond recovery? Not at all! Rather, because of their transgression, salvation has come to the Gentiles to make Israel envious. But if their transgression means riches for the world, and their loss means riches for the Gentiles, how much greater riches will their fullness bring!... For if their rejection is the reconciliation of the world, what will their acceptance be but life from the dead? (Romans 11:11-12, 15)

In other words, if non-Jews in the early church were dramatically impacted by only a small portion of the Jewish population recognizing Messiah, what will it look like when "all Israel" is transformed by the tender touch of Jesus? Paul doesn't mince words here; he states that it will be life from the dead. That is, we will see the most dramatic revival the world has ever known. Millions will "come to life," having formerly been dead to the things of the kingdom. Those once blind will see!

But they will not be alone.

THE FAMILY

Let's use this example. If you were going to hire one of us for a vital position in your company, you would certainly want a résumé, references, and no doubt a face-to-face interview. This is standard procedure. Yet many key positions assigned within both the corporate and governmental worlds are offered as a result of prior connections. We all recognize the power of connections. We feel more confident hiring those we either know directly or close friends of close friends. This is quite natural.

Let's say, however, that you were given the opportunity to interview the candidate's family. And, for our analogy's sake, you are somehow assured that the insights you cull from these family members are guaranteed as unbiased and factual. Who wouldn't want this opportunity? Nobody really knows a man like his wife or kids, or even his parents. The family assessment is certainly the most significant in terms of its ability to bring to light true character. Sadly, this opportunity is not available within the corporate world.

But what if, in the world's assessment of Jesus, they were able to get a snapshot of Jesus directly from his bloodline? For centuries, millions of Gentiles have streamed into the kingdom of God, even though the majority of Jesus' "family" have rejected the One these millions have chosen to follow. Now, what if there was a dramatic and apparent reversal in the way the biological family viewed their Son? This assuredly would have an impact on the world's view of Jesus.

This, we believe, is the essence of Paul's reasoning. If the Jewish dismissal of Yeshua as Messiah by God's sovereignty resulted in so many Gentiles' acceptance of that same Son, then the native family's acceptance must lead to a kind of mass awakening! Is this too hard to fathom? Let's see if we can find support for this within the ancient writings of the prophets.

THEY UNDERSTOOD THE PRINCIPLE

Part of the calming effect that occurs within those who choose to enter the red door of life is a function of recognizing that God has the whole show under control. He is sovereign and is not distracted by daily headlines or large-scale events. His Word is steadily and unceasingly moving toward fulfillment.

Of course, this necessitates him first having a plan.

God's plan has always been singular in focus——restoration of man to himself for the sake of his glory. To accomplish that, he could have taken any number of courses. But for whatever reason, God deemed it critical to first reveal himself to a specific group of people, in a specific "place," in a specific way, and at a specific time. He chose Abraham, making him the very first Jew. God told him to go to a place west of the Euphrates and east of the Mediterranean (a place he would show him when he got there). He made a very clear covenant with Abraham about 4,000 years ago. Why the Lord chose Abraham as the progenitor or established covenant with him in the Middle East at the time that he did, we do not know. He just did! He chose Abraham and his descendants to carry the weighty task of bringing blessing to the world. Awesome——God's choice, God's time, God's way and God's place!

Understanding God's sovereign choice, we should not be surprised to discover that he would hint at his plans beforehand. When God chooses to declare his plans before they occur, he is unequivocally supporting his claim to be outside of time and space. Every other religion in the world claims divine guidance. No religion other than the faith revealed within the Jewish prophets and consummated in Jesus has an ongoing record of fulfilling prophecy after prophecy in the unfolding of its story. In other words, God proves himself as God by allowing us to peek into the future, then ordaining and occupying the events that fulfill that future. This applies not only to Messianic prophecies, but to all prophecies of Scripture. God inhabits the future as easily as the present or the past.

So, when the prophets expound on a somewhat veiled future, they are planting concepts in the text that often only future generations will fully recognize. One of those concepts or principles is that as Israel is transformed spiritually, they will uncork a blessing of such immense magnitude that the nations will respond. Jeremiah saw this principle and exclaimed:

> "If you will return, O Israel,
> Return to me,"
>
> > declares the LORD,
>
> "If you will put away your detestable idols out of
> my sight
>   and no longer go astray,
> and if in a truthful, just and righteous way
>   you swear, 'As surely as the LORD lives,'
> *then* the nations will be blessed by him
>   and in him they will glory."
> (Jeremiah 4:1-2, emphasis added)

Notice that the restoration of Israel and the blessing of the nations depends on the Jewish people swearing in truth, justice and righteousness. These three elements are all decisive depictions of Jesus. It was Jesus who claimed to be, "…the way, the truth and the life" (John 14:6). It was Jesus—proclaimed to be the Messiah—who would proclaim justice to the Gentiles in fulfillment of Isaiah 42 (Matthew 12:18). It was Jesus who became to us God's righteousness (1 Corinthians 1:30). So, when the Jewish people begin to find themselves declaring these three things together, they will have embraced Yeshua as their Messiah. They will have discovered that righteousness cannot be attained through the law, but must be discovered by entering through the red door of Jesus' atoning blood. As this entry begins, the nations will take note and follow them. As we have said and will continue to say, this has already begun. This is occurring in our day!

But Jeremiah was not alone. Zechariah too foresaw and

prophesied this principle of believing Israel bringing the blessing of God to the nations:

> "The seed will grow well, the vine will yield its fruit,
> the ground will produce its crops, and the heavens
> will drop their dew. I will give all these things as an
> inheritance to the remnant of this people. As you have
> been an object of cursing among the nations, O Judah
> and Israel, so I will save you, and you will be a bless-
> ing. Do not be afraid, but let your hands be strong.
> (Zechariah 8:12-13)

Zechariah also saw a very unique day when men from various
nations would actually see a Jew as someone who God was
actively engaged with. They will be witnessing this outpouring
of God's Spirit on Israel and desire to be part of it.

> This is what the LORD Almighty says: "Many peoples
> and the inhabitants of many cities will yet come, and
> the inhabitants of one city will go to another and say,
> 'Let us go at once to entreat the LORD and seek the
> LORD Almighty. I myself am going.' And many peoples
> and powerful nations will come to Jerusalem to seek
> the LORD Almighty and to entreat him.'
> This is what the LORD Almighty says: "In those days
> ten men from all languages and nations will take firm
> hold of one Jew by the hem of his robe and say, 'Let
> us go with you, because we have heard that God is
> with you.'" (Zechariah 8:20-23)

This amazing time in Israel is often pushed into a millennial
reign of Jesus. But if we see the second coming of Jesus as an
awesome and radical time in history, we cannot imagine that
his literal, physical return will leave men "wondering" where

God is. This minimizes the overwhelming nature of the second coming. So we suggest that we are already entering a time where believing Jews will be met by inquiring Gentiles who desire to know the God of Abraham, Isaac, and Jacob—the God who is Yeshua. When Jesus comes to reign, people will not be ignorant of where to look for him—but they are now, and they will latch on to anyone who they think can authentically point the way to him.

Isaiah also foresaw this kind of seeking of God—and finding him among the Jews:

"Arise, shine, for your light has come,
　and the glory of the LORD rises upon you.
See, darkness will cover the earth,
　and thick darkness is over the peoples,
but the LORD rises upon you,
　and his glory appears over you.
Nations will come to your light,
　and kings to the brightness of your dawn."
(Isaiah 60:1-3)

Here again, we see nations following the lead of a Jewish spiritual regeneration. As the glory of the LORD begins to manifest itself upon the nation of Israel in more and more significant ways, it will be a compelling time. Many will enter the red door in line with physical Jews from around the globe.

INCREASING GLOBAL TENSIONS

It should be pointed out here that when we speak of global impact through Jewish believers, we don't suggest that the entire world comes under the sovereign rule of Jesus prior to his return. We are keenly aware of Jesus' warning that nearing the time of the end, many people's love would grow cold.[33] We anticipate heightened tensions in the Middle East right alongside the incredible bonding between Arab and Jewish believers. Change never comes easy. And in the Middle East, you can expect military battles to emerge during this time of transition. In fact, we would argue that these increasing tensions in the region will be one of the catalysts that inspire both Israel and the surrounding nations to look up to the God of Abraham, Isaac and Jacob.

How all of this unfolds, we cannot say with certainty. But there is a more visibly clear path today than ever before. We pray that you would ask the Lord what his plans are for the people he is preparing to lead this amazing witness to the Messiah in the years ahead—believing Jewish people. In fact, God told Cyrus, who was instrumental in being used by God to help the Jewish exiles return and rebuild the Jerusalem temple, that he could actually ask God about the things concerning the future of Abraham's descendants.

> "Ask Me about the things to come concerning My sons, and you shall commit to Me the work of My hands." (Isaiah 45:11, NASB)

We believe that this is still God's heart. He is open to being asked about how we should endeavor to help the living stones in Israel (Jewish believers) rebuild their temple—not a temple made with human hands, as if God could be constrained to such a place, but a temple built with live human stones. Will we rise along with Cyrus and help in this building process, or will we forgo this unique and thrilling assignment with which we have been entrusted?

REASONS TO CARE

"Why concern ourselves with all of this?" some might ask. "After all, if God is going to spiritually regenerate the nation of Israel, then he will do it in his time."

Our answer to that is simple. If this doesn't strike you as something of great significance, we cannot force you to think it so. We have met with many passionate people of God who are fully engaged in expanding the kingdom who have not embraced these ideas. They continue to invest themselves in the primary work in front of them—bringing fame to Jesus' name every day—but don't see this is as a priority. How foolish we would be to judge such acts of faith!

We, however, see involvement in the spiritual regeneration of Israel as a tactically shrewd move. It seems everyone is always praying for and speaking about the desire for a global revival. What if the key to a global revival rests with the ancient people of God? Is it not correct that God's covenant with Abraham included "I will bless those who bless you, and whoever curses you I will curse"?[34] If so, when we bless the physical descendants of Abraham, the blessing returns to us through them. If you are engaged in kingdom advancement in any arena, it is likely that your most intense desire is for revival among the people to whom God has turned your heart—what a blessing that would be for you! For us, we can imagine no better way to bless the Jewish people than to work alongside the many Messianic Jews whose heart is to reach their brothers and sisters with the incredible news of God's power through the Messiah. And when their hearts are turned to Yeshua, how blessed we really are. As Paul wrote to the Thessalonians: "For now we really live, since you are standing firm in the Lord."[35]

Finally, a second encouragement is this: spiritually emergent Israel is one of the most prophesied events in the Bible.

As we see this happening in our lifetime, we can only say that it deepens our faith in extraordinary ways. Because we live in a cynical and skeptical world that constantly denies what we know to be true, it is radically refreshing to see God's eternal plans still being accomplished. He is self-evident in the rebirth of the nation of Israel, the return of its people, and now the unfolding convergence of believing Jews with believing Gentiles in the advancement of God's plans for the earth. This is the "one new man," and it is as significant a prophetic sign as any we know of!

The present fulfillment of prophecy is a powerfully compelling argument at any time, but especially as we enter a chaotic world. It challenges those who would casually dismiss the people of Jesus as myth-believing fanatics. It forces the issue. How can these things be coming to pass against all odds? This demands an answer.

THE CHAPTER IN REVIEW

Global Impact of Jewish Restoration

ONE BIG IDEA

Jewish restoration beginning in Israel will have far-reaching spiritual impact from the Middle East outward. In this way they become the "blessing" of the Abrahamic covenant.

KEY POINTS

• *The Jewish people are Jesus' own family, and when they begin to broadly attest to his Messiahship, their testimony will carry extra weight.*

• *The essence of the message of the Messiah that the Jews will carry will declare him to be the ultimate bearer of truth, justice and righteousness.*

• *Although many will be impacted by the Jewish testimony, tensions will increase according to Jesus' own prophecies regarding the end times.*

• *If the temple God is building now is a temple made of living stones, we should find great satisfaction in coming alongside the Jewish people who are turning to him and testifying about him.*

9 THE ROLE OF GENTILES IN MINISTRY TO JEWS

IT IS OUR GREATEST HOPE THAT IF YOU HAVE read with us this far, your heart resonates with the possibilities of believing Jews and believing Gentiles uniting in the work God has given us together for the time of revival to come.

If you are Jewish, you carry a heritage of tragedy in your heart. Within the lifetimes of many Jews still living——and of course their descendants——the experience of the Holocaust in Germany before and during World War II has functioned to deliver an abiding fear to an entire group of people. Even in America, some Jewish survivors of the Holocaust have kept their Jewish identity hidden for decades, afraid that another like Hitler will rise to power again, persecuting and killing Jews in the many corners of the world.

Other Jews have made every attempt to "move on," but in doing so they have abandoned their faith in God. They cannot allow in their minds for a God who could have permitted such a horror to descend upon "his people." While many of these Jews have made tremendous contributions in the economic, scientific and entertainment sectors, the spiritual price has been great. Now secularists, these Jewish friends and neighbors have in the most significant way possible forfeited the rich ancestry of their people—they have no place for God in their beliefs and practices.

How can this not break the hearts of Gentile believers, especially those who understand that God's "lineage of salvation" runs first through the Jews, then to the Gentiles? How can we not be aghast at the actions of our fellow Gentiles, who would in some ways declare themselves "religious" but then unleash such violence against any one people, let alone the chosen of God? And how can we not also be burdened for the souls of those Yahweh has called for centuries but who have now decided that he must not even exist if such wickedness could be dispensed on the earth?

Fortunately, there are those Jewish people who have seen the truth of Yeshua's Messiahship—of his sacrifice of love and his death-defying resurrection. These Jewish believers are glad to have brothers and sisters in Christ among the Gentiles, and they are forgiving of those who have wrought harm in the past. They know that Moses, the great prophet and leader of the Old Testament, was lifted up by God even though he had murdered another man. They know as well that the apostle Paul was himself a murderer of the first Jews who dared to trust Yeshua, yet he was restored by God and fortified for ministry to the Gentiles. With a combination of forgiveness and excitement in their hearts, they are eager to join hands with all their fellow believers in the work of sowing and reaping among Jews who have yet to turn their hearts to Yeshua.

Not always in a book that discusses Scripture and theology do you encounter definite practical directions for how you can come alongside Christ in the ministry of his kingdom. We are glad, however, that the Scriptures do point toward some specific ways that Gentile believers can enthusiastically yet sensitively take up the task of bringing Yeshua to Jews who have been choosing a different course to this point in their lives.

REMOVING THE STONES

The prophets spoke more than once of a highway into a lasting place with God. It is both an intriguing and an exciting picture. Look:

Then will the eyes of the blind be opened
    and the ears of the deaf unstopped.
Then will the lame leap like a deer,
    and the mute tongue shout for joy.
Water will gush forth in the wilderness
    and streams in the desert.
The burning sand will become a pool,
    the thirsty ground bubbling springs.
In the haunts where jackals once lay,
    grass and reeds and papyrus will grow.

And a highway will be there;
    it will be called the Way of Holiness.
The unclean will not journey on it;
    it will be for those who walk in that Way;
    wicked fools will not go about on it.
No lion will be there,
    nor will any ferocious beast get up on it;
    they will not be found there.
But only the redeemed will walk there,
    and the ransomed of the Lord will return.
They will enter Zion with singing;
    everlasting joy will crown their heads.
Gladness and joy will overtake them,
    and sorrow and sighing will flee away.
(Isaiah 35:5-8)

What a road! Revelation's promises of "no more mourning or crying or pain"[36] deeply echo the words recorded hundreds of years earlier by Isaiah. A time of immense and lasting joy is coming for those who walk in the Way Isaiah described (what a wonder, too, that the early church referred to themselves as followers of "the Way"). But there is sadness in this passage as well, for we recognize that some will be absent from this road, choosing another course, one without redemption.

When we consider the mind of the non-believing Jew, we see that their hope for walking this road is based on an adherence to their chosen place in Yahweh, apart from the work of Yeshua. Their hope for salvation rests in their national lineage or their adherence to the Law (or both), while both believing Jews and Gentiles recognize redemption as the product of Yeshua's work done on our behalf. The step from non-belief to belief in Yeshua as Messiah can be a giant one—especially when Yeshua has been for so long directly connected with "Christians," those who have in too many cases opposed Jews, even unto their death. If "all Israel" is going to be moved to receive Yeshua as Messiah in faith, an important sowing work needs to begin as soon as possible. We call this "removing the stones."

And it will be said:
"Build up, build up, prepare the road!
  Remove the obstacles out of the way of my
    people." (Isaiah 57:14)

Pass through, pass through the gates!
  Prepare the way for the people.
Build up, build up the highway!
  Remove the stones.
Raise a banner for the nations.

The LORD has made proclamation
  to the ends of the earth:
"Say to the daughter of Zion,
  'See, your Savior comes!
See, his reward is with him,
  and his recompense accompanies him.'"
They will be called the Holy People,
  the Redeemed of the LORD;
and you will be called Sought After,
  the City No Longer Deserted. (Isaiah 62:10-12)

There is preparation that must be done in order to prepare the hearts of God's people to have "eyes to see and ears to hear." God has entrusted that work to us, to those who already believe in Yeshua as Messiah. But we believe the work of sowing (preparation) belongs chiefly to the Gentiles, while the work of reaping (preaching unto salvation) belongs chiefly to those Jews who already believe. In this chapter, we are emphasizing the work of the Gentile believers; in the next chapter, we will look at the work of Messianic Jews.

The first action of the Gentiles, then, is to take part in "removing the stones"—that is, in eliminating the obstacles that stand in the way of Jewish acceptance of the Messiah who has already come. Here are those obstacles:

Anti-Semitism

Without question, the greatest obstacle to a Jewish desire even to investigate the claims of their Messianic fellow-Jews is the legacy of anti-Semitism that has been displayed through the centuries of the Christian Church. Of course, we are referring here to the Christian Church apart from believing Jews— namely, the Roman Catholic Church, especially beginning with Constantine, and continuing through the Reformation into the

Protestant forms of the Church. Virtually all major forms of Christianity through the centuries have given voice to an anti-Semitism that has been hurtful to the Jewish people and destructive to their serious consideration of the Good News of Jesus Christ.[37] Sadly, men like Adolf Hitler, though possessing no real faith of their own, have commandeered Scripture, giving the most dreadful acts of anti-Semitism a certain Christian attachment, making this perception of the extent of Christian anti-Semitism both gravely real and nearly immutable.

But nothing is impossible for God! So while some applications of anti-Semitic thought may be inaccurate or exaggerated, those of us who would see the rise of Jewish belief in Yeshua should function instead as though the perception is dead-on. Certainly, the offense many Jews have felt and continue to feel is real. Therefore, one of our best diffusers of this perception is sincere and ready apology. What would be the effect if every Gentile follower of Jesus, upon meeting a Jewish person—be they believing or non-believing—said something like this, "I want you to know that I have spent a lot of time considering the history of the Jewish people, particularly in the last century. And I just want to tell you how sorry I am that so much tragedy has happened to your people. And more than that, I want to tell you, as a believer in Jesus, how sorry I am that so much of that wickedness has been done by people who say they are Christians"? Frequently, the initial response would probably be to brush off such an apology—"oh, that's not necessary"—but whether the appreciation for such an apology is expressed graciously at first, no Jewish person can escape later meditation on such an encounter. Then perhaps (prayerfully) their heart will begin to soften toward those who have said, written, and enacted derision if not hatred in their direction for so long.

Replacement theology

This long-existent though recently waning interpretation of the Bible has seized every part of Scripture, even the most Israel-pointed prophecies, for the believing Church. Proponents of replacement theology (or "supersessionism") argue that the Church is now Israel, and all the promises given to the ethnic Jews of the past are meant instead for those who follow Yeshua now.

We have already clarified our own thinking on this matter, particularly in the last chapter, by presenting our understanding of the Jewish revival yet to come and the resulting salvation of "all Israel." We will explain these eschatological (end times) views further in chapter 11, but for now suffice it to say that in the ears of a non-believing Jew, the idea of replacement theology—where Israel is not, and possibly never has been, the elect of God—is an affront of the harshest intellectual and spiritual kind. While we would agree that many of God's ongoing purposes now enfold both Jew and Gentile (as we have clearly discussed), we simply cannot go so far as to rob the Jews of the prophecies that can be taken from them only by clever but unfaithful consideration of Scripture.

This book is our own best effort at removing this theological stone from the path of the Jewish people. If "God's gifts and his call are irrevocable,"[38] as Paul explained to the Romans, we simply cannot go down a path that robs our Jewish friends of their place as God's enduring elect and steals from them the purposes of God that are specific to them. We hope that upon reading this book, your understanding is the same, and your theological approach when thinking about, praying for, and conversing with non-believing Jews insists on the Messiahship of Yeshua but maintains the integrity of both God's promise to work out his salvation plans through the Jews first and to provide for them richly in the age to come.

New Testament "bias"

Without question, the evangelical church of the past 75 years has been a New Testament-heavy church. There is much good, of course, born of the emphasis on biblical studies and solid Bible teaching, but explicitly and implicitly too many teachers have veered away from the riches of the Old Testament as "boring" or "difficult" or "Old Covenant" when held up against the texts of the New Testament.

To a non-believing Jew, however, the Old Testament (or Tanakh) represents the entirety of God's expression to humanity. Moreover, Jesus and the apostles frequently pointed to the Old Testament histories, psalms, and prophecies in their teachings and writings. And why not? These were Jewish men finding the ultimate truth of the Messiah in the Jewish texts!

If we are to match hearts with non-believing Jews, we need to be versed in the Old Testament. The truth is, among many secularized Jews in the United States and Europe, if you are knowledgeable in the Old Testament Scriptures, you will be more knowledgeable than they themselves are, for while they may on special occasion go to synagogue, they are not regularly studying the words of God to them. Thus, if you can speak with loving reference toward these Scriptures, you can remove another stone in the heart of a Jewish person—in this case, often replacing it with a stepping stone of appreciation that you have taken the time to dig into the roots of their people.

Along this same line, you need to understand as well that it is common among Jewish rabbis to point to the New Testament as an anti-Jewish text, predominantly because certain passages point to the Jewish people as those who crucified Jesus. This application is made in spite of the fact that the passages in question were either spoken or written by Jewish men, and even though they were clearly pointed (in context) toward the Jewish leaders, not all Jews. Still, if we make a strong push for "the truth" in this matter and ignore the Jewish sensitivity toward it, we hinder our own efforts to remove the stones.

Western centrism

Finally, there is the stone of Western centrism, where we see the world from our North American or European perspectives to the exclusion of other parts of the world. Sure, some of this is understandable as a function of pure geography. However, the eyes of the Jewish people are always turned toward Israel (although this has changed somewhat among the current younger generations of Jews). Not a small percentage of Jews send financial support to various enterprises in Israel. Many read Hebrew newspapers, or English-language reports of political and religious developments in the State of Israel and the surrounding countries in the Middle East.

In light of this, Gentile believers must ask themselves a simple question: *How much do I know about Israel today?*

While we do not want to become overly entangled in the many political stances—both overt and nuanced—of the region, we do well to be reminded that God has always used natural means to advance his supernatural purposes. These means include the actions of enthroned and elected leaders of the world's nations. Certainly Jews who have read the Old Testament book of Daniel understand the role of national and international politics and imperialistic endeavors in the lives of their own ancestors. Moreover, they recognize the long lineages of Jews and Arabs traced back to the families of Isaac and Ishmael. Therefore, in the mind of a Tanakh-versed Jew, all political activity, and chiefly such activity in the Middle East, is part of God's ever-flowing stream of action.

So it makes plain sense for Gentiles, too, to gain an understanding of historical and current developments in the Middle East, especially if we are going about the business of removing the stones that hinder relationships between non-believing Jews and Christians, and even more between non-believing Jews and the Christ. Read the newspaper, explore the Internet, and begin to learn about the developments affecting the State of Israel. Your ability to converse with traditional Jews on these matters—even if you do not agree with all of their political positions—will help open further avenues of conversation.

PRAYERFUL 'WATCHMEN'

In the days when cities built walls to protect their inhabitants, the role of watchmen—set atop the parapet to look for invading armies—required soldiers of incessant attentiveness. A lack of vigilance could mean the destruction of one's city, and the death of one's family, friends, and neighbors.

It was the image of the watchmen to which Isaiah appealed when, in conveying the LORD's promise to restore the Jews to their land, he said:

> Listen! Your watchmen lift up their voices;
>   together they shout for joy.
> When the LORD returns to Zion,
>   they will see it with their own eyes. (Isaiah 52:8)

and

> I have posted watchmen on your walls, O Jerusalem;
>   they will never be silent day or night.

You who call on the LORD,
    give yourselves no rest,
and give him no rest until he establishes Jerusalem
    and makes her the praise of the earth.
(Isaiah 62:6-7)

These watchmen—and certainly in the application for our time, these will not be limited to men!—are those whose voices are lifted in watchful, even constant prayer for the coming glory of the LORD in Jerusalem. Their hearts are melded with the LORD's in his desire and his purpose, for his people to be brought back into their land for the purpose of salvation.

We believe, of course, that this salvation comes only through faith in Yeshua, but as we have laid out through the course of this book, a return of Jewish people, both non-believing and believing, to Israel will come first. It is for this return that the "watchmen" pray, urging the LORD to enact his work among the Jews, knowing that the joy will be theirs to share when this happens. We, then, contribute as Gentile believers to the plan of God when we add our vigilant prayers to the mix on behalf of the Jewish people.

GENEROUS TRANSFERENCE OF WEALTH

Most Gentile believers are familiar with the concept of financial giving, bringing tithes and offerings to their church, supporting foreign and domestic missionaries, and donating to benevolence ministries working among the poor and needy. And, as we noted earlier, many Jewish people give as well, with particular interest in supporting the continuing development of the State of Israel. But Jews are not alone in benefitting Israel through their financial support. Over the past 60 years, since the reestablishment of Israel as a nation, Christians too have directed hundreds of millions of dollars toward ministries in Israel. We are glad for this, seeing it as a fulfillment of prophecy:

> Then you will look and be radiant,
>   your heart will throb and swell with joy;
> the wealth on the seas will be brought to you,
>   to you the riches of the nations will come.
> (Isaiah 60:5)

More than that, we see it as a continuing of the tradition established by the early believers on behalf of their Jewish brothers and sisters in Christ:

> Now, however, I am on my way to Jerusalem in service of the saints there. For Macedonia and Achaia were pleased to make a contribution to the poor among the saints in Jerusalem. They were pleased to do it, and indeed they owe it to them. For if the Gentiles have shared in the Jews' spiritual blessings, they owe it to the Jews to share with them their material blessings. (Romans 15:25-27)

It is a great privilege to continue to honor our Jewish brothers and sisters in this way! However, we know that dollars directed to spurious destinations are not going to advance the kingdom purpose God has in mind. The truth is that believing Jews are often persecuted for their faith in Yeshua. It is hard to watch money that was meant for the good of all Jews in advance of a hoped-for Jewish revival be used to benefit those who would stand against belief in Yeshua.

Therefore, in the spirit of shrewdness that Jesus commended among his followers, we would encourage you to be generous toward our Messianic Jewish brothers and sisters, but to do so with discernment. By giving to Messianic Jewish missions in Israel, we can be more certain that this kingdom money is being used to feed the poor, care for prisoners, and love the people of the land in the name of Yeshua. In this way, we depart from a Zionism that would support the State of Israel in any sense; rather, we want to send financial support in advance of the coming Spirit-work of God among his people.

FELLOW UNDERSHEPHERDS

In chapter 6 of this book, we wrote extensively of the work of Messianic Jews as the prophesied shepherds to God's people—shepherds who would lead them into truth, with abundant care. Of course, these are men and women who recognize Yeshua as the Great Shepherd and understand their role as "undershepherds" to him, serving the people as the Holy Spirit gives them faith and gifting.

Many such Gentiles have also been raised up by God's Spirit, and they have the ability to bless not only fellow Gentiles but believing and unbelieving Jews as well. No Jew is comfortable with the term "conversion"—in the same way that people of nearly all faiths rankle at the word. But when people are addressed with care for who they are (which is the role of a shepherd), their hearts become increasingly open to the things that fill the hearts of those caring for them. This may require literal years of sowing kindness and equity in conversation, the result of which the caring shepherd may never see on this earth. But this is a work that we can do in preparation of the coming revival.

Remember, we are speaking of branches that have been bruised and sometimes broken off the vine. In their hurt, they may not be open to the preaching of an outsider. But twice over Isaiah speaks of the ministry of foreigners among the Jews,[39] tending and caring for their places and their people. Done well, in the spirit of Christ, this kind of shepherding, vinedressing work can help open doors to salvation.

A PRIVILEGED LINEAGE

In closing this chapter, we take pleasure in commending our Gentile brothers and sisters to the work of an exceptional lineage. We have already written of "the Gentile test," where we saw that many non-Jews were brought by God to align themselves with and bless the Jewish people. We consider this a path of privilege, for if many professing Christians in the past have looked down upon, insulted, and even abused God's elect, what an excellent calling and work it is to go forth instead with the truer love of Yeshua!

Consider Cyrus, the Persian king of Judah's exile to Babylon who paved the way for the rebuilding of Jerusalem and the temple. Long before Cyrus' rise to power, Isaiah prophesied that this Gentile king would be instrumental in assisting God's people; God said that he would "raise up Cyrus in my righteousness; I will make all his paths straight."[40] In fact, Cyrus proclaimed: "The LORD, the God of heaven, has given me all the kingdoms of the earth and he has appointed me to build a temple for him at Jerusalem in Judah."[41] Now there is a man who knew his calling! His ensuing actions equipped Ezra to begin leadership of this important and tangible pro-Israel work. We would suggest that the greater work in our time is to build avenues for the advancing development of living stones that will be brought together in the construction of God's "spiritual house to be a holy priesthood, offering spiritual sacrifices acceptable to God through Jesus Christ." We would also assert that our modern day Ezras are our Messianic brothers and sisters. Whatever we do to support these people and their kingdom work comes in the line of Cyrus.

Consider also Ruth, the Moabite widow who famously told her Jewish mother-in-law, "Your people will be my people and your God my God." For Ruth, a type of salvation literally came to her through the Jews. Naomi counseled Ruth in how she might find favor with Boaz, one who would be her kinsman redeemer in an Old Testament type of Yeshua himself. It was from this marriage that David and eventually Jesus himself made their natural descents. The blessings that came for Ruth came because of her staunch commitment to the Jewish people and through their blessing her in the way of the Abrahamic covenant (that the Jews were blessed to be a blessing to the nations).

And finally, consider the Canaanite woman of Zarephath, as told of in 1 Kings 17. This woman, down to her final meal, agreed in faith to "first make a small cake of bread" for the Jewish prophet Elijah——this, when she had only enough for herself and her son. In agreeing to help the bedraggled and famished Jewish prophet, this woman received a most remarkable blessing as well. God's miraculous hand did not allow her "handful of flour in a jar and a little oil in a jug" to expire; they carried her through until the next rains. More than that, through Elijah, the LORD raised her dead son back to life.

God has long honored those who have loved and provided for the Jewish people. It was no accident that the first visit of the Holy Spirit to a Gentile home was at the household of Cornelius, for even as a Roman centurion stationed in Israel, Cornelius was known for his generosity to the Jews and his fear of their God. Now it is our turn, as Gentiles in a world growing increasingly hostile again toward the Jewish people. We cannot stand silent as many did in the time of the Holocaust and the pogroms of history. There is too much at stake. As the number of Jewish brothers and sisters we have in Yeshua increases, our neglect of their well-being would not only be a disgrace to the unity of the Spirit of which the Christian church so frequently speaks, it would endanger the ancient elect of God as well.

We cannot speak confidently of "the day and the hour," for Jesus was clear that when it comes to prophecies, these are known to no man. We do not know who among us, if any, will live to see Pentecost 2, though that would be a wonderful reward for those who stand with the Jewish people now. But if our lives are eternal as we know them to be, then on this side of death or the other side, we will want to know the fullness of rejoicing when that day comes. If we have taken pains—perhaps quite literally—to honor and serve the Jewish people in this lifetime, we will experience that celebration with unbridled happiness.

THE CHAPTER IN REVIEW

Role of Gentiles in Ministry to Jews

ONE BIG IDEA

Those who love God should love and respect the Jewish people, desiring their salvation and seeking to enable the spread of the Good News of Jesus among them.

KEY POINTS

• *Gentile believers should endeavor to "remove the stones" that hinder the path of Jews to God. These hindrances include anti-Semitism, replacement theology, New Testament "bias," and Western Centrism.*

• *We should seek to become diligent "watchmen," praying for revival to stir among the Jewish people as they come in contact with those bearing the love and message of Jesus.*

• *We should consider the level to which we might give financially in support of believing Jews who are looking to extend the Good News of the Messiah among their fellow Jews.*

• *When God opens the door, we should take the opportunity to minister alongside our Jewish brothers and sisters in word and in deed. This is our privilege as those who share the lineage of faith that comes from and is given to our heavenly Father.*

10 THE ELISHA MINISTRY
IN EXPECTANCY OF THE COMING AGE

THE CONFRONTATION BETWEEN THE HEBREW prophet Elijah and the prophets of Baal described in 1 Kings 18 remains one the most well-known accounts in all of Old Testament Scripture. Its combination of drama, humor, and the miraculous captures readers' attention and places them in the position of many modern sports fans: rooting for a winner.

Add this dramatic episode to the other miracles of Elijah's ministry, culminating in his being taken up into heaven on a chariot of fire, and you quickly grasp why Elijah has been revered throughout both Jewish and Christian traditions.

And yet, we maintain another question: *What has happened to Elisha?*

You may recall from your reading of the Old Testament histories that a fascinating exchange took place in Elijah's final days between the aging prophet and his protégé, Elisha. Here is the most essential content of that exchange:

> The company of the prophets at Jericho went up to Elisha and asked him, "Do you know that the LORD is going to take your master from you today?"

"Yes, I know," he replied, "but do not speak of it."

Then Elijah said to him, "Stay here; the LORD has sent me to the Jordan."

And he replied, "As surely as the LORD lives and as you live, I will not leave you." So the two of them walked on.

Fifty men of the company of the prophets went and stood at a distance, facing the place where Elijah and Elisha had stopped at the Jordan. Elijah took his cloak, rolled it up and struck the water with it. The water divided to the right and to the left, and the two of them crossed over on dry ground.

When they had crossed, Elijah said to Elisha, "Tell me, what can I do for you before I am taken from you?"

"Let me inherit a double portion of your spirit," Elisha replied.

"You have asked a difficult thing," Elijah said, "yet if you see me when I am taken from you, it will be yours—otherwise not."

As they were walking along and talking together, suddenly a chariot of fire and horses of fire appeared and separated the two of them, and Elijah went up to heaven in a whirlwind. Elisha saw this and cried out, "My father! My father! The chariots and horsemen of Israel!" And Elisha saw him no more. Then he took hold of his own clothes and tore them apart.

He picked up the cloak that had fallen from Elijah and went back and stood on the bank of the Jordan. Then he took the cloak that had fallen from him and struck the water with it. "Where now is the LORD, the God of Elijah?" he asked. When he struck the water, it divided to the right and to the left, and he crossed over.

> The company of the prophets from Jericho, who were watching, said, "The spirit of Elijah is resting on Elisha." And they went to meet him and bowed to the ground before him. (2 Kings 2:5-15)

The "spirit of Elijah" ꞏre accurately, the anointing of the Lord on the ꟷhad been trans- ferred from the ꞏ ꞏwho re- mained. Moreov ꞏome, the blessing giv ꞏ Elijah had known! Sc ꞏstion— why has Elija' ꞏtten, ex- cept by tho' ry fashion that leads t' counts?

We be' and that the answer] eologians can agree, t ꞏine of the Old Testan e Old Covenant and t contentious, and he ꞏ e same way Elijah ha꞉ ose of two separate co꞉.. And yet this was the type of messꞏ. de the coming of the Messiah, Yeshua.

This is also why Jesus markeᴅ ꞏ ꞏr dividing line between John's life and ministry and the lives of all those who would follow him into the kingdom. Recall that Jesus stated in Matthew 11:11, "Truly, I say to you, among those born of women there has not arisen anyone greater than John the Baptist; yet he who is least in the kingdom of heaven is greater than he." Jesus was suggesting that though John's ministry was extraordinary, it would not compare with even the least in the new kingdom—those who would enter through the red door. This blood covenant would make way for the coming of the Holy Spirit on a permanent basis within the life of a believer. John, though great, could not function in this kind of renewed life because he perished before this new life was made available through Jesus' death.

We know that the Messiah's death and resurrection ushered in a New Covenant, whereby faith became the law of salvation. Faith was counted as righteousness because it depended wholly on the righteousness of Christ, the Righteous One. This truth, championed throughout the history of his church, means that so much has changed since the days of John the Baptist, in the same way that so much changed when the mantle of prophecy was passed from Elijah to Elisha.

In our estimation, if Jesus is to be ushered in to His eternal reign by the cry of the believing prophets, it will be done with a different spirit, a different tone. It will be done with its basis in grace, rather than the Law. It will be done in the life-giving pattern of Elisha. It will be done in concert by the full body of believing Jews and believing Gentiles. And, we believe, it will be done in preparation for the end times.

That said, we would like to unveil for you the types of this "Elisha ministry," as they are seen through the accounts of Elisha himself in the book of 2 Kings. You might say that what you are about to survey could be titled, "The Defining Characteristics of the Elisha Generation."

Some will ask as they read how we can draw such meaning from what might be called "histories" rather than "prophecies" of the Old Testament. For one, we know that among the prophets whose words were recorded as "prophecies," God called for actions of allegorical (and prophetic) meaning—Ezekiel ate a scroll, Isaiah walked naked among the people, Hosea married an unfaithful woman. Also, we find examples of such application among Paul's writing. For instance, in his letter to the Galatians, Paul drew from the historical accounts of the children of Hagar and Sarah (Ishmael and Isaac) to explain what was being fulfilled in his own day: a separation between those enslaved to the law and those made free sons of righteousness through Yeshua. Surely the acts of a "double blessed" prophet such as Elisha can not remain locked in "the annals of history." Though it may require a way of thinking that is somewhat new for you, we invite you to find contemporary and future prophetic meaning in the accounts of Elisha's ministry. This is not a "new meaning" or a "new way of looking at things," as you might find among some theologians who essentially rewrite Scripture in the way they interpret it for our time. Rather, this is the realization that the same ideas that have been held captive in history may have been intended by God to be unveiled in a future time. We believe that future time is now. As you read, we wonder if you won't be convinced of the same.

A MENTORED READINESS

As we have already briefly seen, Elisha was made ready for his ministry by serving faithfully under his "master," Elijah. This relationship was no different than many others that have existed throughout time, with one experienced person mentoring another with less experience. This mentoring is intended to prepare the protégé for the various situations that can test one's faith, resolve, and giftedness in the Spirit of God. And there is no substitute in this type of training for time spent with the one who is doing the teaching.

When, in 2 Kings 2:14, Elisha took the cloak of Elijah and struck the Jordan just as Elijah had done some minutes before, the waters again divided and Elisha returned to the other side.

As testified to by the company of prophets who witnessed this miraculous event, Elisha carried with him "the spirit of Elijah." These prophets recognized not only that Elijah's role of "God's leading prophet" had been passed on to Elisha, but that the essence of Elijah's prophetic ministry had been given to Elisha, too.

In the present age, as we look around us, we see the same sort of mentoring arising within local churches and individual believers whose hearts are turned to the instruction of Jesus as Lord. With the Spirit of God himself resting on these intent believers, much can be done in his power for his kingdom. Beyond this, we are especially excited to note that a particular group of these believers has "crossed the Jordan," reentering present-day Israel, the Eastern boundary of which is formed by the Jordan itself. These people are our Messianic brothers and sisters, those anointed to do strategic work among the many non-believing Jews who even now are also returning to the land. With a "double portion" of the blessing carried by John the Baptist, the herald of the Messiah's first coming, these Spirit-infused believers will lead the heralding work of the Messiah's eternal glory and reign. Gentile believers like ourselves would do well to serve as "the company of the prophets," confirming and following their lead.

BAD WATER TURNED GOOD

Many of the accounts that give us a picture of the work of Elisha are brief vignettes of miraculous moments. While the miracles are exciting in themselves, the nature of these accounts is often odd, as they are quickly delivered and frequently offer little context or resolution. What we know from studying the prophets, however, is that God not only spoke through their words but through their actions. So we must ask ourselves what meaning God could have been trying to convey through the miracles done through Elisha. This is not a hunt for "ghosts," where a deeper meaning must be squeezed from the text at all costs. Rather, it is an awareness that the Scriptures are best approached when we inquire of God himself as to their meaning. What has resulted from this hopeful and honest search for us are prophetic meanings for our own time and kingdom work; in all cases, including the present one, we believe that the message from God that arises through these seemingly random accounts are well within the boundaries of what God presents to us through the Scriptures. We pray that you agree.

In 2 Kings 2:19-21, a group of city leaders come to Elisha with a concern for their town (Jericho). While the location of the city is ideal, they tell him, the water is bad and the land is unproductive. Here is the ensuing action of the prophet:

> "Bring me a new bowl," he said, "and put salt in it." So they brought it to him.
> Then he went out to the spring and threw the salt into it, saying, "This is what the LORD says: 'I have healed the water. Never again will it cause death or make the land unproductive.'" And the water has remained wholesome to this day, according to the word Elisha had spoken.

What a wonderful blessing God provided to the people of Jericho through Elisha! But if you are like us, you must wonder if God included this account in Scripture for any particular reason. We do know that if you read through the progressions of the lives of Elijah and Elisha, you will find that the Bible includes exactly twice as many "miracle stories" for Elisha as it does for Elijah—the double blessing![43]

What we are convinced of is this: the people of the Messiah will be known in the time ahead as those who "give fresh water."

Many Old Testament readers will be familiar with the bitter water of Marah, arrived at by Moses and the Hebrew people in the Desert of Shur (Exodus 15:22-26). The people cried out, "What are we to drink?" In response, Moses cried out to God, "and the LORD showed him a piece of wood. He threw it in the water, and the water became sweet."

We would not be the first to point you here toward a parallel between this miracle of God in the desert and the work of Christ on the cross. For instance, consider these rich words of the 19th Century preacher Charles Spurgeon:

> And now, today, contemplating His atoning sacrifice, and by faith resting in Him, the troubles of life and the troubles of death are sweetened by His dear Cross, which, though it is a bitter tree in itself, is the antidote for all the bitterness that comes upon us here and hereafter. That remedy was most effective. When they cut down the tree, and put it into the water, it turned the water sweet—they could drink it!
>
> And let me assure you that in the case of our trouble the Cross is a most effective sweetener. Shall I put the tree into the water for a minute, and then ask you to drink? Have you been suffering pain, or any other form of tribulation? I will let the Cross soak in it for a minute, and your first reflection will be—"In all this that I am called to suffer there is not even a single particle of punishment for my sin! God has punished Christ. Consequently He cannot punish me—to punish two for one offense would be unjust—therefore there is nothing penal in all that I am suffering."

The Elisha ministry of bringing fresh water into the place where the water has before been undrinkable, then, is most definitely a work given to those who carry the Good News of Jesus, believing Jews and believing Gentiles.

In the prophecy of Jeremiah, we find invaluable reference to bad water. Look:

> "For the LORD has doomed us to perish and given us poisoned water to drink because we have sinned against him." (Jeremiah 8:14)

Here Jeremiah's prophecy was as the words of the people spoken about the punishment God had brought upon them according to their sin. The LORD lamented that his people bore no shame over their sin, so he pronounced an attention-getting judgment of famine, pestilence, and the poisoned water. No one can receive salvation without first recognizing his sin and a humble contrition before God, yet it is often the contrast between the goodness of "fresh water" and the shame of "poisoned water" that allows one to see the need for salvation. Indeed, Paul wrote to the Romans that it is God's kindness that leads to repentance. Our willingness to bring the Good News of Christ, as those who carry clean water from a distant source or offer to dig a deep well, aligns us with the Elisha ministry in Jesus' name.

Consider as well that there are those who would make it difficult for others to see God. They are those who would stir up dissension or speak falsehood. Here is a helpful passage from Ezekiel:

> "As for you, my flock, this is what the Sovereign LORD says: I will judge between one sheep and another...Is

it not enough for you to drink clear water? Must you also muddy the rest with your feet?" (Ezekiel 34:17-18)

That is, there are some who come to God with good intent for themselves, but who make the going impossible for others. Such was the case with the Pharisees. Religious leaders frequently begin their journey toward God honestly; they really desire to know him. But through the generations, the Pharisees traded empowerment by God for earthly power. They created roadblocks of legalism and elitism that "muddied the waters" for those who came after them. Similarly in our time there are those whose religious structures and exclusionary theology make it difficult for people to see God. Here, those of us who take pleasure in the Messiah can offer a shortcut to God in this sense: "For there is one God, and *one mediator between God and men, the man Christ Jesus,* who gave himself as a ransom for all men—the testimony given in its proper time" (1 Timothy 2:5-6, emphasis added).

Finally, we would be remiss if we did not note two teachings of Jesus himself that heighten the ministry of turning bad water to good in the lineage of Elisha.

First, in the Sermon on the Mount, Jesus said, "You are the salt of the earth. But if the salt loses its saltiness, how can it be made salty again? It is no longer good for anything, except to be thrown out and trampled by men" (Matthew 5:13). Here we make connection between the salt that Elisha put into the water to make it clean again and the salt Jesus would have us use to "season the world" with the message of salvation.

Second, there is the well-known encounter of Jesus at the well with the Samaritan woman, told in John 4. The water from this well, he said, would only leave her thirsty in time.

She would be compelled to come again. What he had to offer instead was water that would become in its partaker "a spring welling up to eternal life."

The ministry of Elisha, then, brings life where life is waning away. It is easy to see even in a cursory glance at the world an increase in wickedness; yet at the same time we read often of people turning to the Messiah in masses, even where the resistance to him has been greatest. Keeping the Messiah to ourselves is like hoarding fresh water when all the world around us is dying of disease due to contaminated water sources.[44]

THE END OF FALSE GOSPELS

If the preceding Elisha episode of providing fresh water to the people of Jericho seemed brief and a bit out of place, the passage that follows it in 2 Kings 3 is more curious still:

> From there Elisha went up to Bethel. As he was walking along the road, some youths came out of town and jeered at him. "Go on up, you baldhead!" they said. "Go on up, you baldhead!" He turned around, looked at them and called down a curse on them in the name of the LORD. Then two bears came out of the woods and mauled forty-two of the youths. And he went on to Mount Carmel and from there returned to Samaria.

What on earth is going on here? This question, while expressing incredulity, also energized my (Jeffrey Cranford's) inquiry of the Lord over this passage for some time. For one, Elisha's ministry is in no other place marked by such judgmental confrontation, though Elijah's ministry frequently was. And even if Elisha did mete out acts of judgment as his master had done, this seems shockingly extreme. For a bit of teenaged antics these youths were mauled by bears? What kind of prophet is this, and what kind of God does he serve?

We find our answer in a couple passages with close parallels to this one. First, there is this warning in the Jewish Law:

> "If you remain hostile toward me and refuse to listen to me, I will multiply your afflictions seven times over, as your sins deserve. I will send wild animals against you, and they will rob you of your children..." (Leviticus 26:21-22)

The youths, though immature in their dealings with Elisha, were certainly hostile to him, showing contempt for his person and his role.

Now consider a second passage. It closes the books of Chronicles, which account for the reigns of the kings of Israel and Judah. In this final section of these books, the fall of Jerusalem at the hands of the Babylonians is reported—but only after this:

> The LORD, the God of their fathers, sent word to them through his messengers again and again, because he had pity on his people and his dwelling place. But they mocked God's messengers, despised his words and scoffed at his prophets until the wrath of the LORD was aroused against his people and there was no remedy. (2 Chronicles 36:16)

Just as the youths who had mocked Elisha had been cursed and punished for their jeering, the nation of God was sent into exile for their derision of God's prophetic messengers. And herein lies the essence of this third component of the Elisha ministry for our time and the time to come: false gospels will be brought down, doomed to destruction. Of course, this is good news, for it will undergird the Good News. We would say that we are even encouraged by some of the argumentation of the "New Atheists," for against them excellent apologetic argumentation is also being heard, and we know that God will guard closely the truth that is his alone.

Before we leave this matter, let us also explore several passages from the New Testament that confirm for us the importance of this aspect of the Elisha ministry. We'll begin with 1 Corinthians 15:12:

> **But if it is preached that Christ has been raised from the dead, how can some of you say that there is no resurrection of the dead?**

Here the apostle Paul was pointing to the single greatest hinge upon which Jesus' Messiahship swings, his resurrection. Of Jesus' resurrection, Paul wrote that our faith is "futile...if Christ has not been raised." So it is understandable that he would confront in his letter to the Corinthians those who would dismiss this essential truth. No false doctrine robs the hope we proclaim like the claim that Jesus was not resurrected, so Paul adamantly argued against such teaching.

Next, we turn to a second of Paul's letters, Galatians. In the opening verses of that epistle, we find these strong words:

> **But even if we or an angel from heaven should preach a gospel other than the one we preached to you, let him be eternally condemned! As we have already said, so now I say again: If any-**

> body is preaching to you a gospel other than
> what you accepted, let him be eternally con-
> demned! (Galatians 1:8-9)

Not only do these words cry out for the veracious continu-
ance of the one gospel of Jesus as Messiah, they echo the Old
Testament passages we reviewed that advance a cry for judgment against those who deny the ultimate truths of God and
his Son.

Finally, we point to words of Jesus that have confounded
commentators and teachers for centuries:

> And so I tell you, every sin and blasphemy will
> be forgiven men, but the blasphemy against the
> Spirit will not be forgiven. Anyone who speaks a
> word against the Son of Man will be forgiven, but
> anyone who speaks against the Holy Spirit will
> not be forgiven, either in this age or in the age to
> come. (Matthew 12:31-32)

Although we can speak no more definitively than the many
others who have offered insight into what Jesus meant by "the
blasphemy against the Spirit," we do want to offer this suggestion. Could Jesus have been delineating between the work that
he was doing on earth as the incarnate Son of God for a fixed
period of time and the ongoing work of God on earth throughout time via the Holy Spirit? Could Jesus have been saying that
it is one thing for doubters to call into question the historicity
of his life and work, but quite another for them to advance
arguments against God as he lives and acts among us? In our
minds at least, this certainly fits the context of an Elisha ministry in our time and going forward. People who doubt that

God is working among us and speaking through us—as the youths did with Elisha and the nation did with the succession of other prophetic messengers of God—are in grave danger of eternal judgment for their argumentation and unbelief against *the living God.*

THE WORLD IGNORED AND WORSHIP EMPLOYED

The next account we draw from Elisha's prophetic role in 2 Kings is somewhat longer and assists us in understanding two important aspects of the Elisha ministry in preparation for an explosion of faith among Jewish people.

The king of Israel (the northern of the two Hebrew kingdoms), Joram, was seeking to settle a score with the king of Moab. In order to strengthen his forces, Joram appealed to Jehoshaphat, who was the king in the southern Hebrew kingdom of Judah, and Joram allied with the king of Edom. These men were quite different in their obedience to God. Joram followed in the line of idol-worshiping kings in Israel, while Jehoshaphat maintained the ways of the LORD among his people. Therefore, when it came time to make strategic decisions regarding this battle, which appeared hopeless for the Hebrew kings, it was Jehoshaphat who stepped up and determined to call upon a "prophet of the LORD." This call was sent to Elisha, and Jehoshaphat confirmed that "the word of the LORD is with him."

When the kings went down to meet Elisha, however, the prophet made one thing clear: he was dealing with these men only because Jehoshaphat was among them. He knew that Jehoshaphat alone among the three feared and served the LORD. Elisha fiercely delineated between what was holy and what was common, and he would have nothing to do with the latter. Likewise, we believe that the Elisha ministry now being formed will become staunchly opposed to the presence of any idolatry that would turn eyes, ears and hearts from the One True God.

After clarifying why he was continuing to assist these kings, Elisha delivered his initial instruction: "Bring me a harpist." Elisha revered the musical worship leaders that God perpetually raised up among his people. God has designed us and desires us to be worshipers and singers in our expression of faith and praise to him. Elisha understood this and ordered music to be played as he waited to hear from the LORD. And indeed we read, "While the harpist was playing, the hand of the LORD came upon Elisha and he said, 'This is what the LORD says: Make this valley full of ditches. For this is what the LORD says: You will see neither wind nor rain, yet this valley will be filled with water...'"[45]

The next morning, water came flowing in from Edom to fill the ditches that had been dug according to Elisha's instruction from the LORD. The land was filled with water, down into these ditches. Across the lines, the Moabite soldiers readied their arms and came out for battle. When they looked across the land and saw the sun on the water, it appeared red, like blood, in their eyes. They assumed that the unified kings had battled among themselves and that this was the blood of all their men; now the plunder was there for the taking! But when the Moabites came across the land unprepared to fight, the Israelites routed them, chased them back into their land, and destroyed their cities.

In our time, we see an increase in the appreciation for worship music, honoring God both in instrumentation and Jesus-honoring lyrics. The church has seen a significant push toward spirited worship in recent decades. Not only has musical worship been employed at the "heart level" in local churches around the world, but earnest discussion about authentic worship in all aspects of life has arisen among church leaders. And Jesus-focused worship is one of the beautifully unifying characteristics within the Middle East today. Jews and Arabs are now coming together to worship Jesus through song and dance.[46] How good it is to see God moving among his people in this way! How good it is to partner with him in employing such worship! True worship always ushers in the presence and voice of God for direction both personally and corporately.

We are convinced that the prophetic picture offered through this event in Elisha's ministry reveals to us all that a life of worship, regularly and reflectively employed, digs "ditches" which God can fill with the fresh water of his own work among us. In the Elisha ministry rising even now and moving forward, we believe that worship—coupled with a steadfast adherence to holy endeavors that honor God alone—will be a vital component of the empowering of God's people for his purposes.

WORKING IN CONCERT WITH THE HOLY SPIRIT

At the outset of the fourth chapter of 2 Kings, we are treated to a recount of a woman in desperation and the miracle of God that saved her. The woman, a widow, faced the terrible prospect of one of her creditors coming to take her sons as slaves to settle the debt. As her husband had been one of the company of prophets, she knew Elisha and cried out to him regarding her horrifying circumstances.

Elisha said that he would help her and asked the woman what she had in her house. She replied that she had only "a little oil."

Elisha sent the woman out to collect empty jars from her neighbors. Specifically, he told her, "Don't ask for just a few."

After collecting the jars, she returned to her home as Elisha had instructed her and closed the door behind her and her sons. Then she began pouring her oil into the many empty jars, setting aside each one as it was filled. In this way, she filled all of the many jars that she had collected, and when the last one was full, the oil stopped flowing. Elisha then told her that she could go and sell all the oil and settle her debts. More than that, there was money left over for her and her sons to live.

Consider this amazing account in conjunction with Jesus' words to the inquiring Pharisee, Nicodemus, in John 3: "For the one whom God has sent speaks the words of God, for God gives the Spirit without limit." Throughout Scripture, oil is symbolic of the Holy Spirit. But many operate as though the Spirit is limited and that they must guardedly cling to what he has implanted in them. No! What God has always intended for his people is to give away their blessing. This is the core principle of the Abrahamic Covenant—"you are blessed to be a blessing"—and it confirms the nature of the Holy Spirit, at work in continuing abundance. When Jesus was speaking to Nicodemus of "the one whom God has sent," he was speaking specifically of himself. But his words about the Spirit's infilling of God's servants can apply to each one of us, especially as we allow for him to miraculously flow in us with ever-increasing abundance. God will provide for all our needs and the needs of others through us. Those who engage in the Elisha ministry will lay hold of this principle in mind and in action.

INSIGHT AND HUMILITY REWARDED

The account of the Shunammite woman begun in 2 Kings 4:8-37 is particularly touching because the spirit of this woman is so insightful and hospitable, and her response to blessing is filled with humility.

Perceiving the godly calling on Elisha's life, this woman arranged with her husband to build a small room where Elisha and his servant Gehazi could stay when they were in her area. Elisha was grateful for this kind act and asked what he might do for the woman. The woman modestly expressed that she had no needs, but Gehazi pointed out the woman and her aging husband had no son. Elisha received a promise from the LORD that he passed on to the woman: within a year she would have a son. The woman was amazed by this kindness of God, but sure enough, the child arrived.

When he was a boy out in the field with his father, however, he fell suddenly ill, and by the time he was returned to his room in the house, he could only sit in his mother's lap, where he died. Quietly, the woman set forth with a servant at her side to find Elisha and tell him of her anguish. At the woman's insistence, Elisha returned with her to her home, where he prayed to the LORD, then literally breathed life into the boy.

The woman's story is then interrupted for a time, but we pick it up again at the beginning of 2 Kings 8. Here Elisha warned the woman of an impending famine. Upon his advice, she moved her family to "the land of the Philistines" for seven years. When the time came for her to return and seek the return of her lands via the king's decree, God's timing was perfect. In the hour that she arrived, Gehazi was meeting with the king and regaling him with news of the many miracles that had been done through Elisha's ministry. When the woman entered the king's court, she became an instant party to the testimony of God's miracles, and the king gladly restored to her her family's land, even offering her the money that had been earned from her land in her absence.

These accounts point to an important aspect of the Elisha ministry—that God both gives and honors insight to people he loves, and he rewards them even in the midst of difficult times.

In this case, that reward included the preservation of the Shunammite woman's family and her family holdings.

Consider this idea in the light of Paul's words to the Corinthians:

> Godly sorrow brings repentance that leads to salvation and leaves no regret, but worldly sorrow brings death. See what this godly sorrow has produced in you: what earnestness, what eagerness to clear yourselves, what indignation, what alarm, what longing, what concern, what readiness to see justice done. At every point you have proved yourselves to be innocent in this matter. (2 Corinthians 7:10-11)

Certainly our Jewish friends have known sorrow throughout the generations, and perhaps most severely in the past century. Unfortunately, some Jewish theologians have converted this sorrow into unbelief, not able to see what God might be doing through such tragedy. The "Elishas" who see God's hand even in troubling times, however, recognize that there is much to be gained by turning our sorrows over to God and allowing him to work with excellence in us, producing aspects of character that could be developed in no other way—chief among these being humble surrender to him.

This is a message that is carried best, of course, by Jews among Jews. Jewish men and women who believe in God and his Son Yeshua firmly bear within themselves the evidence of God's work through trial. They may also be able to personally testify to the miraculous work of God in their health, homes, and businesses. They can show how God has preserved their families against all odds. In this way, the Elisha ministry is a ministry of hope, offering through God what no earthly promise can deliver. And those who engage in this ministry—as well as those who provide for this ministry—will joyfully receive God's blessings.

NEUTRALIZING BAD THEOLOGY

In 2 Kings 4, we come across another brief miracle account, one with no apparent meaning other than the physical aid it provided. In Gilgal, famine seized the land, and the company of prophets scrounged for whatever food they could find. One day, one of the servants prepared a stew made with herbs and gourds collected in the wild. But when the stew was prepared and tasted, a cry went up among them: "O man of God, there is death in the pot!" The men were expressing their hunger and their desperation to Elisha. Although there may have been more urgency in the moment, the account as we read it shows Elisha flatly giving the simplest of directions: "Get some flour." Sure enough, when the flour was added to the pot, the "death" was neutralized and the stew was safe to eat.

Under normal circumstances, we might present this passage without further discussion. Perhaps that would be the right thing to do. But because we have recognized the many other aspects of God's working both then and now according to the events of Elisha's life, we cannot pass over this miracle without asking whether God has something more for us to see here.

In seeking the Lord on this matter, we were compelled to consider three prophetic passages that contain verbiage similar to the words used to tell the story of the death in the pot. Look at these with us:

You have forgotten God your Savior;

> you have not remembered the Rock, your
>   fortress.
> Therefore, though you set out the finest plants
>   and plant imported vines,
> though on the day you set them out, you make
>   them grow,
> and on the morning when you plant them,
>   you bring them to bud,
> yet the harvest will be as nothing
>   in the day of disease and incurable pain.
> (Isaiah 17:10-11)

> I had planted you like a choice vine
>   of sound and reliable stock.
> How then did you turn against me
>   into a corrupt, wild vine? (Jeremiah 2:21)

> "Go through her vineyards and ravage them,
>   but do not destroy them completely.
> Strip off her branches,
>   for these people do not belong to the LORD.
> The house of Israel and the house of Judah
>   have been utterly unfaithful to me,"
>   declares the LORD.
> (Jeremiah 5:10-11)

In each of these prophetic passages, we find reference to a vine or plant intended for good by God that had turned to corruption, wildness, unfaithfulness and "nothing." These turnings were abandonments of the truth about God himself, the kind of abandonment that leads to spiritual death.

Similar faithless theology continues into our time, when

God is either dismissed altogether or replaced by death-producing spiritual pursuits of false gods and false ideas. Would it not make sense, then, that a key aspect of the Elisha ministry would be to neutralize bad theology with the life-giving truths of Scripture?

One interesting note: The natural reaction in the case of this bad soup would have been to throw it out. Instead, Elisha's direction—a sort of let's-work-with-what-we've-got instruction—was in keeping with Jesus' parable of the wheat and the tares. The tares were not to be ripped out on the spot but allowed to grow alongside the wheat. In both cases, we are implicitly encouraged to recognize the difference between true brothers and false teachers. There is no perfect theology, of course. We will all miss the mark of God on particular points of reasoning. But when we make a habit of appealing to the well-founded truths of Scripture, we effectively rebuke false elements in our own thinking and in the teaching of others, whether their intent is for good or for evil.

Although the account given to us in 2 Kings 4 may have been intended initially as a narrative of a miracle, it would certainly fit the context of God's design for his kingdom and for the spiritual climate of our time. We should generate from this narrative an impetus to be truth-bearers in a world where falsehoods kill. This is a ministry that believing Gentiles and believing Jews can engage in together, as bearers of the light of the Messiah.

OVERCOMING ANTI-SEMITISM

We have already written of the need for Gentile believers to make strong intentional efforts to eradicate anti-Semitism from our churches and seminaries first and then from our greater communities (see the "Removing the Stones" section of chapter 8). If we are to take our lead from the record of Naaman in 2 Kings 5, we would find this to be an aspect of the Elisha ministry as well.

Naaman, you may recall, was a commander in the Aramean army. He was also stricken with leprosy—which may have been the actual disease itself or a similarly annoying affliction of his skin (the ancient Hebrew for this word is ambiguous). One of Naaman's wife's servants was a girl captured from Israel, and when she heard of Naaman's disease, she suggested that he go see Elisha. Through a series of ambassadorial transactions, Naaman found himself face to face with Elisha's front door. A messenger emerged from the house and told Naaman that he should wash himself seven times in the Jordan River in order to restore his flesh. Though perhaps an odd suggestion to Naaman's ears, it was tame enough. But it was not the kind of reception or prescription Naaman was looking for, and it caused him to declare superiority for his own country and people over that of Elisha the Jewish prophet: "Are not Abana and Phapar, the rivers of Damascus, better than any of the waters of Israel? Couldn't I wash in them and be cleansed?" Naaman's anti-Israel bias was showing.

But the commander's servants rose up out of love and respect for their commander and suggested that Elisha's direction was not so very difficult. Naaman heard the wisdom in their words, went down into the Jordan, dipped himself seven times and emerged a clean man. It should be no surprise that Naaman was pleased with this result, but his response was actually filled with repentance. Listen to his words upon receiving his healing: "Now I know that there is no God in all the world except in Israel."[47]

Compare for a few moments this exchange between Naaman and Elisha with the exchange between Jesus and the Samaritan woman at the well. We already recounted this story in chapter 3. Jesus, unmistakably a Jew, surprised this woman by addressing her directly and asking her for water. In the conversation that ensued, the woman's hesitancy toward the Jewish people—though perhaps deserved in the midst of the adversarial relationship between Jews and Samaritans of the time—showed in this expression: "Our fathers worshiped on this mountain, but you Jews claim that the place where we must worship is in Jerusalem."[48]

Into our time, greater and lesser anti-Semitism rears its head in the beliefs, words and actions of non-Jewish people everywhere. Some of this might be dismissed as what is common between people of different backgrounds—like the banter between neighbors in New York City boroughs. But horrifying genocidal wars and tyrannies, rooted in differences of skin, heritage, and religious expression in such places as Ireland, Bosnia, and Rwanda (all in our lifetimes), point to the fact that we can never allow such racism to take even the smallest root in our hearts. And when we are speaking specifically of God's people of promise, the Jews, we do well to use every resource we have—be it prayer, conversation, intellect, advocacy, teaching, or other avenues—to help incorporate the Elisha ministry of overcoming anti-Semitism in ourselves and help others see as well the ongoing need for respect of the Jewish people.

GETTING OUR CUTTING EDGE BACK

The sixth chapter of 2 Kings opens with another short account of a seemingly incidental miracle. The company of prophets sets out to build shelters for themselves. But during the endeavor, one of the men's axhead flew off its handle and sunk into the Jordan River. The man cried out, for he had borrowed the ax. Elisha was called and he quickly recovered the axhead.

Here's how: He cut a stick and threw it into the water near where the axhead had gone in. The axhead floated to the top of the water, and the man who had lost the axhead reached out and recovered it.

This account carries a powerful symbol with ramifications for the Elisha ministry. Remember that Elisha himself was not a prophet whose oracles were recorded in Scripture, as were those of others, such as Isaiah, Jeremiah, Ezekiel and Daniel. Rather, both Elijah and Elisha conducted prophetic acts, revealing both the miracles and the mystery of God. In the case of the floating axhead, two symbols are most evident, according to their prevailing appearance in Scripture. The first of these is water, which is often linked with the word of God: "...Christ loved the church and gave himself up for her to make her holy, cleansing her with water through the word."[49] The second is the symbol of the cut-off stick. Throughout Scripture, we find this pointing to the Jews who have been separated from God.[50] Now consider this wonderful possibility: When the Jewish people who have been separated from God by their adherence to the Old Covenant come in contact with the living Word who is the Messiah Yeshua (and who is revealed through the full word of God included in the New Testament), they will get their cutting edge back. That is, they will be restored to their full calling and receive the fullness of the gifts God has for them.

WALKING ACORDING TO THE UNSEEN AND MERCY

The next account we cross in Elisha's life demonstrates, among other things, the difference between the judgment-strong ministry of Elijah and the grace-strong ministry of his protégé. In 2 Kings 6:8-23, we read of the frustration of the king of Aram, who could not successfully engage the armies of Israel, because they kept anticipating his plans and avoiding his own soldiers. The king of Aram assumed that there was a spy among his officers, but the officers were aware of the truth—that Elisha was supplying the Israelite army with a unique form of reconnaissance. "Elisha, the prophet who is in Israel," the Aramean men reported to their king, "tells the king of Israel the very words you speak in your bedroom." In other words, the LORD had given Elisha prophetic ability to see the unseen.

So the king of Aram changed his focus; he pursued Elisha in the city of Dothan. The Arameans surrounded the city. Fear entered the heart of Elisha's servant, Gehazi, who saw the assembled armies and asked Elisha what could be done.

Elisha's response revealed his prophetic insight. He told his servant, "Don't be afraid. Those who are with us are more than those who are with them." Then Elisha asked the LORD to reveal to Gehazi the LORD's own assembled armies—there were hills full of horses and chariots around them.

Elisha next asked God to strike his enemies with blindness. When their sight was taken away, Elisha spoke to them, telling them that this was not the city they were looking for. When they asked him to lead them to that city, Elisha marched them right into Samaria, where they found themselves standing before the king of Israel.

The king made an assumption that most of us would have made, asking Elisha if he should go ahead and kill these Aramean soldiers.

But Elisha instead instructed the king to feed them plentifully and send them on their way. After it is reported in 2 Kings 6:23 that the king of Israel had done this, we read this fascinating conclusion: "So the bands from Aram stopped raiding Israel's territory."

We find powerful meaning in this account as it relates to the

Elisha ministry for our time and the time to come.

First, we are amazed by the spiritual insight of Elisha, and his ability to see with spiritual eyes what others could not. This is a God-given ability that Paul wrote about to the Corinthians, when he said, "For our light and momentary troubles are achieving for us an eternal glory that far outweighs them all. So we fix our eyes not on what is seen, but on what is unseen. For what is seen is temporary, but what is unseen is eternal."[51] Those who walk closest to God are always given the ability to see things with his eyes, according to the Spirit and not only according to the flesh (or the physical eyes we have been given). In Elisha's case, he was able to see things that drove out fear and brought the confidence of hope.

Second, we are delighted to see the mercy dispensed by Elisha, even against men whose original design was to kill him. And we are more delighted still to see the outcome of that mercy: the end of the enemy's persecution. How in keeping this is with the words of Peter, who wrote:

> But in your hearts set apart Christ as Lord. Always be prepared to give an answer to everyone who asks you to give a reason for the hope that you have. But do this with gentleness and respect, keeping a clear conscience, so that those who speak maliciously against your good behavior in Christ may be ashamed of their slander. (1 Peter 3:15-16)

In the Elisha ministry, hope and mercy will be coupled as agents of the reconciliation we can offer to those who have yet to say yes to Jesus. In fact, we are dispensing Jesus' very own instruction: "Love your enemies."

Third, perhaps most thrilling of all is that believing Jews and believing Arabs are already offering this kind of mercy ministry to one another in Israel. Where much is made in the media of "peace talks," these brothers and sisters in the Messiah have already been practicing peace by ignoring their ethnic backgrounds and typical political stances in favor of unity in Yeshua. This can only happen when those in Jesus see what is unseen—the love of God for others—and endeavor to render expressions of that same love to one another.

Before moving on, let us make one other note here. The king of Israel, when he addressed Elisha, called him "my father." The political leader—whose own heart was not true to Yahweh, by the way—reverentially deferred to the spiritual leader, Elisha. Could it be that while the political leaders of our time may or may not be servants of the Messiah, they will increasingly and respectfully seek guidance from those who do have the Messiah because these leaders know in their spirits that this is the best available counsel in the world?

THE OUTCASTS LEADING THE WAY

The next event recorded in the life of Elisha may be the climax of all we have been relating with regard to the ministry of believers in the end times. You would do best to read the entirety of the passage, 2 Kings 6:24-7:20, for yourself, so that you are aware of all the details. Here, though, is an overview, with specific reference to some of the prophetic pictures we will discuss with pertinence for the Elisha ministry.

At a point later in the life of Elisha, Samaria was surrounded in a siege tactic by the entire Aramean army, and the people of Israel were starving within the walls of the city. We are shown the severity of this starvation in two ways: (1) by the testimony of a woman who had engaged in the cannibalism of her own son, and (2) by the astronomical prices of two noted foods, donkey's head and dove's dung.

The king of Israel expressed outrage at matters, directing his ire at Elisha, whom he held responsible for the famine because the man of God had not urged the LORD to alter the circumstances. The king sent messengers to Elisha, telling the prophet that he was aware that the distress was from the LORD, and that he was no longer going to wait for the LORD, which was a threat to kill Elisha and move on to other gods.

Elisha then prophesied that the following day would bring entirely different circumstances. Food would be plentiful and the inflationary economy would be returned to normal. When the king's nearest man challenged the possibility of such a rapid turnaround, Elisha pronounced that this man would see the change but not eat of it.

That evening, a group of four lepers who had been camped just outside the gate of the city decided that they had as good a chance of being fed in the camp of the Arameans as they did by the people of the city. And they rose up and headed toward the Aramean camp. When they arrived, they discovered that the camp had been completely abandoned, with food, clothing, and valuables left behind.[52] The lepers helped themselves twice over, then were struck by the selfishness of what they were doing. They said, "We're not doing right. This is a day of good news and we're keeping it to ourselves." And they returned to the city to report their discovery to the king.

As might have been expected, though, the king and his advisors were cautious. Perhaps these leprous men had been sent as a trap by the Arameans to lure the Israelites from their city and slaughter them. So they arranged to send a scouting party to uncover what the Arameans were up to. But the scouts found that the Arameans had indeed fled en masse, leaving their camp full of all its supplies, and strewing all excess baggage along the road behind them as they went.

Upon this news, the people of Samaria emerged from their city and loaded up on every necessary good from the Aramean camp. Just as Elisha had prophesied, the city's food supply was again replete, and prices returned to normal. Moreover, the king's nearest man had been sent to take charge of the gate, but in this position he was trampled by the flow of humanity and died as Elisha had foreseen—witnessing the fresh abundance but not partaking of it.

With the full account in front of us, and a deepening understanding of God's work among those who would dispense the Elisha ministry in the time leading up to the return of the Messiah, we see an amazing set of symbolic pieces. Consider first these correlations:

Aram = Gentile world
Samaria/Israel = Jewish community
lepers = those cast out by the non-believing
Jewish community (believing Jews)
donkey = stubbornness
dove's dung = lost connection to the Holy Spirit

Now consider the flow of the story again, with these symbols in place. An army of Gentiles has surrounded a group of Jews, feasting off the produce of their land. Though these Gentiles would not be considered "believers," they have access to the simple bounty of earth. That simple bounty, we might say, represents the basic spiritual health that comes directly from the hand of God.

This health once belonged to the Jews, but now it has been taken from them. Why? They have traded it for stubborn adherence to legal strictures and have thereby said goodbye to the true heart of God. Like the people of old, they have tried to sustain their spiritual lives through law-abiding efforts that were never intended to give life. Notice that the Jews in Samaria were eating the heads of donkey (the essence of stubbornness) and the dung of doves (evidence that the Spirit had once been a welcome presence but had been pushed away by faithlessness). This was the normal course of God's people in the Old Testament; they mistakenly abandoned God himself, both for other gods and for the god of their own religious design.

Included in that religious design was the unmerciful exclusion of those who had been deemed unclean, i.e., lepers. While the Old Testament law did call for separation of those with leprosy from those who did not have it—for the sake of the physical health of all people—Jesus noted that the legalistic leaders among the Jews had adhered to the letter of the law without maintaining the spirit of God's own heart, which included justice, mercy, and faithfulness.[53] The lepers outside the gate were reviled in this way.

We have watched the same thing happen today among faithful Jewish people who have furthered their Jewish faith by trusting in Yeshua Messiah. Though these believing Jews are increasingly making *aliyah* and establishing residence in Israel, they have found their beliefs demeaned and their places of worship vandalized. So where are they going to gain support? In the Gentile world, where the provision of God is still to be found.

But look! The exciting aspect of this prophetic narrative is that the lepers, though untrusted at first, are those who lead their people back to abundant life! The Messianic Jews will bring true life in Yeshua to their Jewish brothers and sisters.

And they will be supported in this by resources from the Gentile world, both believing and unbelieving.[54]

The greater Jewish community today is wholly unbelieving, not accepting Jesus as Messiah, but also ignoring the rabbinical teachings of the non-believing Jews. And yet, like the Israelites living in Samaria so long ago, who called on Elisha to provide relief for their dire conditions, these Jews have a "spiritual homing device" deep in their souls. They know they need the living God. The living God took flesh as man who would be resurrected, Yeshua of Nazareth. He is alive today at the right hand of the Father, and together they are preparing the restoration of the Jewish people, to be led by those who now may be outcasts, but who in the years and decades to come will dispense the Elisha ministry with God's heart and by God's Spirit.

GOING 'ALL THE WAY'

We now leap several chapters through the accounts of kings of Israel and Judah to a well-known event at the end of Elisha's life. Jehoash reigned in Israel, and though the king "did evil in the eyes of the LORD," he harbored a great deal of respect for Elisha. We are told in 2 Kings 13:14:

> Now Elisha was suffering from the illness from which he died. Jehoash king of Israel went down to see him and wept over him. "My father! My father!" he cried. "The chariots and horsemen of Israel!"

Though Elisha certainly knew the heart of this king as he knew the heart of others, he responded prophetically to Jehoash, telling the king to fire an arrow out the east window of his room. When the king had done so, symbolizing, according to Elisha, a coming victory over Aram, the prophet then told the king to strike the ground with his arrows. The king did so three times. But here was Elisha's response: "You should have struck the ground five or six times; then you would have defeated Aram and completely destroyed it. But now you will defeat it only three times." The next line then tells us that Elisha was dead and buried. As far as Scripture is concerned, this prophecy to Jehoash amounted to Elisha's dying words.

It is easy, as many interpreters and preachers have done, to draw from this passage inspiration to go wholeheartedly into the work God lays out for each of us. This is not faulty interpretation, for we do know that God desires for us to be hot for him, not lukewarm.[55] But as our survey of Elisha's life has shown, we believe that there is special meaning for the end of days.

For one, we would suggest that no aspect of the Elisha ministry should be set aside or deprioritized in relation to the others. All that we have discussed to this stage should be employed.

Two, we would suggest that there is a role for every believer in the unfolding kingdom of God, and perhaps more especially as the Jewish rebirth approaches. While we know not to "despise the day of small beginnings," we are moving now toward an enlarging climactic end to the work of God as he has long designed it. A few folks here and there setting out to do this work is not enough; God intends to engage all of his people.

And three, we would suggest that a Spirit-infused intensity will mark the true movement forward. A few "love taps" may have done the job in other environments, but these will not mark the work of the people of God in the time to come.

Now let us speak of the arrows themselves, for this is not the only time arrows have prophetic significance in Scripture. We'll consider two passages:

Listen to me, you island;
  hear this, you distant nations.
Before I was born the LORD called me;
  from my birth he has made mention of my
    name.
He made my mouth like a sharpened sword,
  in the shadow of his hand he hid me;
he made me into a polished arrow
  and concealed me in his quiver.
He said to me, "You are my servant,
  Israel, in whom I will display my splendor."
…"It is too small a thing for you to be my servant
  to restore the tribes of Jacob
  and bring back those in Israel I have kept.
I will also make you a light for the Gentiles,
  that you may bring my salvation to the ends of
    the earth." (Isaiah 49:1-2, 6)

A debate can be waged about who is being referred to as "the servant of God" and "a light for the Gentiles" in this passage—Jesus himself or the Jewish people. But if we look to the application of this passage by Paul in the book of Acts, we find dual fulfillment in both Jesus and the Jews. In Acts 13, as we have noted elsewhere, Paul told the believers in Antioch, "This is what the LORD has commanded us," then he went on to quote Isaiah 49:6. But later, to King Agrippa, Paul fixed the same idea upon Jesus alone: "I am saying nothing beyond what the prophets and Moses said would happen—that the Christ would suffer and, as the first to rise from the dead, would proclaim light to his own people and to the Gentiles."[56] We believe it makes perfect sense under these interpretive circumstances that God sent forth the first arrow of salvation to the Jews and to the nations in Jesus, and that he intends now to send a quiver of arrows out for the same purpose: to broadcast the light of salvation.

We make additional appeal to Zechariah 9:12-13, which shows the return of the people Israel for the purpose of empowering blessing that they may effectively carry forth the word of God into the world:

> Return to your fortress, O prisoners of hope;
> > even now I announce that I will restore twice as
> > > much to you.
> I will bend Judah as I bend my bow
> > and fill it with Ephraim.
> I will rouse your sons, O Zion,
> > against your sons, O Greece,
> > and make you like a warrior's sword.

The images are of war, but we are reminded again that the battle is not against flesh and blood. Rather, God intends for the believing Jews, in partnership with believing Gentiles, to bring the light of Christ to Jews first and then to the nations like never before.

The answer to peace in the Middle East does not lie in treaties. It lies in the arrows. As we write, hatred toward the presence of the Jewish people and government is perhaps more violent than ever. Radical Palestinians, Arabs, and Muslims all have announced deadly intentions for Israel and the Jews living there and in other parts of the world. They have fired missiles into the country and detonated bombs within it. Neither peace talks nor strong stands by either side have made a discernible difference in these conditions over the past 50 years. The residents of Israel and its surrounding nations live under threatening conditions daily.

But what if the peace of Yeshua truly took hold among the Jewish people living in the land? What if obedience to the true path of salvation by the Messiah of the God of Abraham, Isaac and Jacob pervaded the land so that the Jewish people became agents of "the more important matters of the law—justice, mercy, and faithfulness"? And what if the reach went out to the east, like Jehoash's arrow, so that it influenced Jordan and Syria and Iraq and Iran? Would we then know the peace of Jerusalem, for which we are told to pray in Psalm 122, and would we hear people in those presently acrimonious lands announce to Israel, "For the sake of the house of the LORD our God, I will seek your prosperity"?[57]

Though we suspect there are only a few reading these words, we must respectfully confront Orthodox Jews here, for these ancient adherents to the Law of God have continually maintained a stance of separation from those outside their religious community. When do these friends in the ancient paths of God intend to engage in the fulfillment of the Abrahamic Covenant—"all the peoples on earth will be blessed through you"—and Isaiah 49:6—"I will make you a light for the Gentiles." Yeshua's words peal loudly: "A city on a hill cannot be hidden." The call of God is there for you turn to Yeshua as Messiah and become the beacon of God with your Jewish brothers and sisters, stepping out into the world to bring the light not to "unclean *goyim*" but to those who need Yahweh as you have needed him. If not now, when?

THE BONES OF ELISHA

The accounts of Elisha do not end with his life. In 2 Kings 13, we are treated to one final miracle.

> Now Moabite raiders used to enter the country every spring. Once while some Israelites were burying a man, suddenly they saw a band of raiders; so they threw the man's body into Elisha's tomb. When the body touched Elisha's bones, the man came to life and stood up on his feet. (2 Kings 13:20-21)

If by this time, you have become accustomed to seeing rich meaning in each of these prophetic episodes, you may wonder along with us what could be happening in this account that has a place in our lives today. This time, however, we would have to admit that the meaning we draw is perhaps more metaphorical than prophetic (not that the two cannot coexist!).

If we are to suggest that the whole explanation of the Elisha ministry as we have laid it out for you in this extensive chapter is the structure of God's work among the Jewish people in the time to come... and if we recognize that the bones are the structure of a human being... then we might say that when a Jewish man or woman comes into contact with the structure of the Elisha ministry, life will spring forth in that person. One who was dead will come to new life in Yeshua! And through thousands of such individual revivals, the structure or "bones" of this ministry will prepare the way for the "Pentecost 2" of which we have already written, and ultimately the return of Jesus.

This is an especially exciting picture in light of two New Testament passages. The first is from the book of Acts, when the apostles were jailed for preaching the Gospel of Jesus.

> But during the night an angel of the Lord opened the doors of the jail and brought them out. "Go, stand in the temple courts," he said, "and tell the people the full message of this new life." (Acts 5:19-20)

It simply cannot be overlooked that this first release of the Gospel after the first Pentecost came with a direction to address the people from the courts of the Jewish temple. And what were they to be told, but "the full message" of the Gospel that brings life!

The second passage comes from Paul's second letter to the Corinthians, where he was describing the essence of the ministry he and his fellow missionaries had been given.

> You show that you are a letter from Christ, the result of our ministry, written not with ink but with the Spirit of the living God, not on tablets of stone but on tablets of human hearts... He has made us competent as ministers of a new covenant—not of the letter but of the Spirit; for the letter kills, but the Spirit gives life. (2 Corinthians 3:3, 6)

Here Paul drew a recognizable delineation between the old life of law-conscious religion and the new life enabled by the release of the Holy Spirit after the ascent of Jesus into heaven. This is the very life available to those who come in contact with believers empowered to render the Elisha ministry.

SOME WORDS ABOUT GEHAZI

Before departing from this chapter, we need to offer some observations about Elisha's long-time servant, Gehazi, for it is in Gehazi that we see some daunting contrasts between the pure nature of the Elisha ministry and a faulty manifestation of that ministry.

Gehazi's attitude and actions were marked by at least five destructive qualities that we might find in false or ineffectual leaders today:

Lack of empathy and kindness

When the Shunammite woman came in distress to Elisha after the death of her son, she took hold of the prophet's feet. We read next that "Gehazi came over to push her away," and Elisha rebuked him for his gruffness (2 Kings 4:27). The fruit of the Holy Spirit—including kindness, goodness, gentleness, and self-control—will be strongly evident in the lives of those who are ministering as Elisha; but those who are not in the flow of this ministry will meet the needy with ill will.

Lack of power or anointing

Immediately after the Shunammite woman explained her plight to Elisha, the prophet sent Gehazi ahead with his own staff, instructing the servant to "lay my staff on the boy's face." But when Gehazi arrived at the woman's home and did what Elisha had told him to do "there was no sound or response." Yet when Elisha himself came, he stretched himself out upon the boy and he was brought back to life (2 Kings 4:25-37). The work of those who function in the flow of the Elisha ministry will be marked by the power and anointing of the Lord, even unto the miraculous, as the Lord ordains. Those who are not functioning in this ministerial flow, however, will see little or no power for ministry of this kind.

Greed

While Elisha adamantly refused to accept tribute from Naaman after the healing of the commander's leprosy, Gehazi secretly trailed Naaman's party and asked for remuneration in Elisha's name (2 Kings 5:15-27). True ministers of God's love always provide service without thought for payment; false ministers will look for a way to fatten their wallet or "improve their lifestyle" in exchange for helping others.

Unclean and uncovered

More frightening is the outcome of Gehazi's greed. Once he had informed Gehazi that he was aware of the servant's willingness to take money from Naaman for himself, Elisha pronounced a curse on Gehazi: "Naaman's leprosy will cling to you and to your descendants forever." Immediately, Gehazi's skin turn white as snow; he was leprous.[58] The Mosaic Law disqualified from priestly duties any who possessed leprosy or another infectious skin disease, until such time as they were clean. If those engaged in the Elisha ministry are the true royal priesthood of God as written of in 1 Peter 2:9, their anointing for the work of God will be righteously attractive both to those who are ready for such ministry and those who are not. However, if a "Gehazi" is unwilling to receive the cleansing of the blood of Jesus, it will be of no matter that he or she walks among those truly in Christ and doing Christ's work; still, he or she will be disqualified. We see New Testament examples of this kind of ineffective involvement by both Simon the sorcerer in Acts 8:9-25 and the seven sons of Sceva in Acts 19:13-16.

It is also worthy of note that Jesus himself spoke specifically of the "many in Israel" who did not receive healing for their leprosy, while "Naaman the Syrian" (a Gentile) did. In the context of his words, Jesus was addressing those of unbelief as contrasted with those of belief—rather than the contrast that the religious leaders wanted to see, which was the difference between privileged Jews and unclean Gentiles. *Will you walk under the covering of the blood of Christ, or will you only try to walk near those who truly do?* There stands the critical question for all people, no matter their earthly origin.

Lack of spiritual eyes

Earlier in this chapter we recounted the events of 2 Kings 6, when Elisha softened Gehazi's fear of the enemy by telling him, "Those who are with us are more than those who are with them." Gehazi could not see the horses and chariots of fire that Elisha saw with spiritual eyes until Elisha asked the LORD to make a way for Gehazi to see them. Likewise, those who minister in the spirit of Elisha will be like the man of God, who could see things in the spiritual realm beyond what can naturally be seen. But those who are not empowered for this ministry will have only their natural eyes with which to see.

CONCLUSION

We have spent extended time covering the material in this particular chapter, because it represents the core of what God has given to us to share with both believing Jews and believing Gentiles as we progress through the kingdom plan of God. Many of the other elements of this book are vitally important to understanding God's intentions for the world and for each of us as believers. But understanding the Elisha ministry gives us a sense of (a) how God has spoken through his prophets from ancient settings right into our own time, and (b) the practical appearance of ministry emphatically and penetratingly released through Spirit-empowered men and women.

Two of the principal components of the pictures given to us through Elisha's original ministry will serve us as we leap forward into our closing chapter, which is an exploration of the implications for eschatology (end times theology) that emerge from all that we have presented here. But before we step into that discussion, we greatly encourage you to ask essential questions of yourself before God:

- Is my heart like Elisha's, devoted to God? Or am I more like Gehazi, interested in the effects of true spirituality but not truly engaged by the Spirit himself?

- Should I seek from the Lord a covering of his blood, that I might be truly cleansed before him and made fit for whatever he calls me to do?

- If my heart is right but I am still desiring maturity, should I be asking God for a new equipping in matters like neutralizing bad theology, walking according to the unseen, or rendering the mercy of God?

It is when we submit ourselves to reflective, challenging questions like these that we humbly open our hearts and our minds to God's best work in us. God, we know, lifts up those who are humble, those who are contrite, those who worship him in spirit and in truth.[59]

Finally, we are compelled to ask one last question, emanating from Matthew 17:9-13, which is comprised of the closing lines of the account of Jesus' transfiguration into his glorified body on the mount with Peter, James, and John:

As they were coming down the mountain, Jesus

> instructed them, "Don't tell anyone what you have
> seen, until the Son of Man has been raised from
> the dead."
>
> The disciples asked him, "Why then do some of
> the teachers of the law say that Elijah must come
> first?"
>
> Jesus replied, "To be sure, Elijah comes and will
> restore all things. But I tell you, Elijah has already
> come and they did not recognize him, but have
> done to him everything they wished. In the same
> way, the Son of Man is going to suffer at their
> hands." Then the disciples understood that he was
> talking to them about John the Baptist.

It is clear, even stated, that the second use of Elijah here refers
to John the Baptist. He had already come; the religious leaders
did not recognize him as the forerunner to Jesus; and he was
put to death by Herod.

But what of the first reference to Elijah—the one who
"comes" ("is coming" or "will come" or "will first come" depending on the translation) and who "will restore all things"?
Could it be that this Elijah is the one who comes in the spirit
of Elijah—that is, as Elisha came? And could Jesus have been
referring to himself, as the one who would restore all things?
And could it be, then, that we, the unified Jewish and Gentile
believers in whom the Lord dwells by his Spirit, carry within us
the spirit of Elisha—a grace-threaded, empowered-for-minis-
try spirit that will carry the light into the darkness? If so, we
have far too often chosen an impotent life when we should be
living and ministering confidently as men and women of God.

THE CHAPTER IN REVIEW

The Elisha Ministry

ONE BIG IDEA

The many acts of Elisha the prophet may be read as pointing to specific acts of ministry in our own time, each serving to expand and enrich the kingdom of God.

KEY POINTS

• *While the prophetic link between Elijah and John the Baptist is widely taught, the ministry of Elisha—who received a double portion of Elijah's blessing—is often forgotten.*

• *Elisha's ministry was decidedly marked by mercy and blessing, much like the ministry of Jesus on earth. For this reason, we have suggested that while an Elijah-John the Baptist heraldry led to Jesus' first coming, an Elisha-type ministry will lay the groundwork for Jesus' return.*

• *Each of the acts in Elisha's prophetic ministry helps us anticipate and understand a correlating aspect of the "Elisha ministry" for our time. These are listed in the chart on the following page.*

• *Elisha's own God-focused spirit was contrasted in the biblical accounts with the self-focused spirit of his servant, Gehazi.*

THE ELISHA MINISTRY

The work of God within and through true believers, both Jewish and Gentile, for the culminating age

. . . .

Mentored readiness • 2 Kings 2:1-17
Upcoming ministers of God prepared for his work by Spirit-led ministers and blessed by God for ministry

Bearers of life-giving water • 2 Kings 2:19-22
Ministers teach of the Messiah's living water

False gospels cursed • 2 Kings 2:23-25
Ministers confront unbelief in teaching and in action

Deep worship and commitment to holiness • 2 Kings 3:1-27
Ministers will depend on worship for clarifying vision
and strength in God to choose righteousness

Appropriate and deliver the Holy Spirit • 2 Kings 4:1-7
Ministers understand the unceasing flow of God's Holy Spirit
and administer his power to those in need

Wisdom and stewardship even in trouble • 2 Kings 4:8-37
Ministers depend on the insight of God for decision making
and for faith, resulting in visible reward (2 Kings 8:1-6)

Neutralize bad theology • 2 Kings 4:38-44
Ministers counter bad theology with biblical truth

Overcoming anti-Semitism • 2 Kings 5:1-14
Ministers lead deep respect for the Jewish people

Restoration of Israel's cutting edge • 2 Kings 6:1-7
Ministers see the return of the Jewish people to a place of
spiritual leadership in the kingdom of God

Walking according to the unseen • 2 Kings 6:8-23
Ministers see things supernaturally, as God sees them

A heart for Jewish restoration • 2 Kings 6:24-7:20
Ministers understand the plight of Jewish lostness and the need for
rescue, even through the hands of "the weak"

Whole-hearted commitment • 2 Kings 13:14-25
Ministers go far beyond the basics to honor God's desires

Firing the arrows of peace • 2 Kings 13:15-19
Ministers elevate Christ as "the peace of Jerusalem"

11 END TIMES IMPLICATIONS

F EW WRITERS SET OUT TO MAKE ENEMIES. IN fact, many idealistically hope that all their readers will come to the same conclusions they have reached. And then there are the people who dare to write about end times prophecy...

We are fully aware that those who are versed in any or all of the various interpretations of the prevailing eschatological systems——namely amillennialism, premillennialism, or post-millennialism——have been compiling a list of questions as they have read this book. And, at the core, these questions are the same. They seek to know whether what we have said coincides with the reader's own way of thinking. Truthfully, we wish this didn't happen. We wish we could have just written about the coming resurgence of the Jewish people and the unity of love for Christ and purpose in mission that is arising between believing Jews and believing Gentiles and avoided discussions of eschatological systems altogether. But that would not be fair to our whole audience, many of whom have a God-wrought interest in end times affairs (maybe even greater interest than our own!).

So we are prepared here to address some of these potential questions. We won't attempt to establish a new system.

In fact, we have reason to respect the work done through the centuries. Theologians of all eschatological persuasions have contributed to our understanding. Moreover, we have been blessed by the contemporary work of "progressive dispensationalists" like Robert Saucy, Craig Blaising and Darrell Bock, who particularly contend (as we do) that Gentile believers do not replace or supplant Israel.

Closer, though, to our own thinking are the open questions of professor Frank Chan at Nyack College, who has proposed a "fourth millennial position" with the growing Messianic Jewish movement in mind. This position, which Chan reluctantly coined as "Jewish restoration postmillennialism" because "no label is totally adequate," allows for a resurgent Jewish people in Christ ahead of Jesus' second coming. We say that Chan's writing includes open questions, which will be our own intent here as well, as opposed to capturing all the loose ends and presenting a completed eschatological system for final consideration or debate. If particular eschatologists are able to take up the study of these matters, comparing them across exegetical work and systematic considerations in an academic way, we (along with Chan) would invite and encourage their work. We are pursuing here a different tack, which is to explore several millennial considerations in a way that communicates reflectively but efficiently with our regular "audiences" where we frequently teach and write—that is, among lay people who are committed to study of the Scriptures but do not have the calling or time of scholars.[60]

Therefore, what we endeavor to do in this chapter is consider some topical items that should both help to address questions of our readers and ask some questions in return. As adherents to the idea of "progressive unveiling" (as discussed in chapter 5), we would suggest that prophetic understanding increases with each generation of believers searching the Scriptures together to make sense of "the signs of the times."

THE QUESTION OF TIME

Let us immediately consider the question of timeframes and timelines. While those who construct systems to show when various end times events will take place normally position these events in linear fashion on a sort of timeline, we would hold absolutely with those who resist any temptation to suggest that "this is the date" of any of these events. This is because we hold absolutely to Jesus' own teaching about his own return, that "no one knows about that day or hour, not even the angels in heaven, nor the Son, but only the Father in heaven" (Matthew 24:36). Jesus himself was subject to his incarnate limitations in this matter, and the secret of its specific time is guarded in heaven. This can present something of a problem for those who are looking to current events as possible clues of scriptural fulfillment. The temptation is great to see not only a closing proximity to the events spoken of in Scripture, but to attach actual dates to these events as well. At times like these, we should both (a) enjoy the hope of the imminent fulfillment of prophecy, and (b) remember that God is sovereign and may yet turn events to achieve a "fuller fulfillment" of his plans.

THE LINCHPINS OF OUR THINKING

Near the close of the last chapter, we mentioned that two aspects of the accounts of Elisha's prophetic ministry serve as essential aspects of our own end times thinking. Let's address these now.

First, there is the account of the Shunammite woman, whose faithfulness to Elisha was lauded before the king by Gehazi in 2 Kings 8:4-5. As Gehazi was reporting this news, the woman walked in, and the king was captivated by her own accounts of the things Elisha had done for her and her family. Now the woman had just spent seven years at Elisha's instruction living in the land of the Philistines. She had come to the king's court asking for the return of her house and land. Joram heard her story with compassion and ordered the return to her of her house, her land, and the income generated from her land in her absence. In the same way, we recognize the merciful return of the land of Israel to the Jewish people in 1948 as a gift from God. Not only is this return of the land not a "future event," as end times events are often regarded as being, but it is now a past event, established and defended for more than sixty years.

But the land is not enough! Understanding that salvation comes only through Yeshua as Messiah, we cannot be convinced that God would return the people to the land without also planning to accelerate the return of their hearts to him. (Here we would definitely depart from those whose "dual covenant" theology would argue that God has provided one path to salvation for the Jewish people and a different path—through Christ—for Gentiles.)

Therefore, the second linchpin of our end times thinking is that there will be a resurgence of faith among the Jewish people as they encounter the love of Yeshua enacted through the many components of the Elisha ministry that we have outlined in this book. Of course, this is entirely the work of God as people are empowered by his Holy Spirit. Seizing upon this work in our own strength or wisdom would produce nothing! This should be exceedingly evident when we are talking about spiritual renewal in a region as religiously divided as the Middle East. Even Jerusalem itself is a hotbed of religious trouble, as Jews, Christians and Muslims all contend for position and power in the city. Peace will not come to Jerusalem—or anywhere else in the Middle East—until Jesus comes to the Middle East. While some would point to the necessity of Jesus' actual return (his second coming) in order for this to happen, we would say that this is happening now. Jesus is returning to Israel, Palestine, and the surrounding nations, coming into the hearts of men and women and children who now see that he alone is Lord. This is not a triumphalistic claim; there is much strife and difficulty still in place in the Middle East. Jesus' physical second coming must still occur for the job to be completed, so to speak. But the "light to the Gentiles" is shining there as it has not done for millennia, if ever. Can we not honor our brothers and sisters, both Jewish and Gentile believers carrying that light, even now?

THE TEMPLES WE ARE

We cannot overstate the importance of a phrase we used just a few lines ago: "Jesus…coming into the hearts of men and women and children." While this is a well-taught and utterly important aspect of faith in Christ—that he indwells us upon our expression of belief in him—it is also frequently forgotten in the midst of discussions that include the question, "When will Jesus come?" We would have to answer this question with most theologians: Jesus' kingdom is both "already" and "not yet." Still, when consideration turns to eschatology, the "already" aspect of Christ and his kingdom are neatly tucked away.

Here's the problem: Jesus will not be tucked away. As we might say of a remarkable athlete confounding the defense of the opponent, he "cannot be contained." Even though he has not yet physically come again, he has established himself by his Spirit in the hearts of all who receive him. And he has equipped these believers by his Spirit to do great works.

Let's consider three remarkable passages here. First, Ezekiel 37:24-28:

> "'My servant David will be king over them, and they will all have one shepherd. They will follow my laws and be careful to keep my decrees. They will live in the land I gave to my servant Jacob, the land where your fathers lived. They and their children and their children's children will live there forever, and David my servant will be their prince forever. I will make a covenant of peace with them; it will be an everlasting covenant. I will establish them and increase their numbers, and I will put my sanctuary among them forever. My dwelling place will be with them; I will be their God and they will be my people. Then the nations will know that I the LORD make Israel holy, when my sanctuary is among them forever.'"

While some theologians see this passage as entirely future in nature, we find ourselves asking too many questions about the present to place ourselves in their camp. Among them:

- *Isn't Jesus already the Good Shepherd?* Certainly, he declared himself to be, adding that his sheep would recognize his voice. Thus, any future "fulfillment" of this prophecy would be no more than a confirmation of what is already true.

- *Don't the laws and decrees reflect the tradition of the Jewish people before God?* The Mosaic Covenant (the Law)

has been replaced by grace in Jesus, but the preponder-
ance of what we might rightly call moral instruction in
the New Testament still communicates God's desire for
righteous living among his believing people. In honor to
the Shepherd who is Jesus, believers everywhere honor
the "laws and decrees" of God in the same way that Jews
have purposed to do since Mount Sinai, but with an in-
ternally responsive motivation rather than an externally
religious one ("circumcised hearts" versus "circumcised
flesh").

- *Are the Jews not already in the land?* Assuming that the centuries of *diaspora* are being reversed in favor of *aliyah,* the
Jews taking up residence in Israel since 1948 have been
enacting this prophecy already. Many more will come,
but this will not initiate the fulfillment of this prophecy
so much as complete it.

- *Hasn't this covenant already been made?* Again, if Jesus himself is the promise of God's peace ("Peace I leave with
you; my peace I give to you" — John 14:27), this covenant was enacted through him and will continue into
eternity as "an everlasting covenant." From this point of
view, a future fulfillment of this prophesied covenant
would be superfluous.

- *What does it mean that the sanctuary is "among them?"* The
wording here—alternately, "in their midst"—is atypical
of wording used for a physical location. Coupled with
Paul's teaching in Athens that "the God who made the
world and everything in it is the Lord of heaven and
earth and does not live in temples built by hands,"[61] re-

quiring that a physical building is necessary for Christ to take residence among us may satisfy our earthbound perspective, but it does not fit other important passages of Scripture.

With that latter question in mind, the second passage that provokes questions about future fulfillment versus ongoing and current fulfillment of Yeshua's lasting residence among us is comprised of his own words recorded in Luke 17:20-21:

> **Once, having been asked by the Pharisees when the kingdom of God would come, Jesus replied, "The kingdom of God does not come with your careful observation, nor will people say, 'Here it is,' or 'There it is,' because the kingdom of God is within [or among] you."**

Here, our prevailing question would be this: Is not the essential component of the kingdom of God the presence of God? If so, while a more literal thousand-year reign of Christ on earth may be established in the future, as our pre- and traditional post-millennialist friends would posit, a most definite work of God through the Holy Spirit is going on in and among us even now. We are in Christ and Christ is in us, and so we must suggest that there is an important aspect of prophetic fulfillment going on even now—it truly is, you see, *progressive* in its course.

Finally, we must also deal earnestly with Paul's expression of the indwelling activity of God as he wrote in 2 Corinthians 6:16-18:

> **What agreement is there between the temple**

of God and idols? For we are the temple of the
living God. As God has said, "I will live with them
and walk among them, and I will be their God,
and they will be my people."[62]

"Therefore come out from them
    and be separate,
           says the Lord.
Touch no unclean thing,
  and I will receive you."[63]
"I will be a Father to you,
  and you will be my sons and daughters,
           says the Lord Almighty."[64]

Paul was advocating a separation based not on Pharisaical
"cleanness" against Gentile "uncleanness" in an attempt to satisfy a distant, judgmental God. Rather, the apostle's argument
for personal holiness was based on the Holy Spirit's residence
in us. It is Christ's presence within us that compels us to honor
him with our behavior—in motivation, in attitude, and in action.

We hope this leads you along with us to wonder aloud why
the "already" aspect of the kingdom of God is often pushed
aside in favor of looks to the future. We cannot, as Jesus said,
bring about the kingdom by even the most careful observation;
we can, instead, access it now. Maybe we would be seizing on
populism to do so, but C.S. Lewis' expression "Aslan [a de-
piction of Christ] is on the move" in his Narnia books might
be appropriately commandeered here. Jews are returning to
Israel—now. Gentiles (including many Muslims) are coming
to Jesus in even the toughest places in the world—now. God
is uniting the two as "one new man"—now. This strongly sug-

gests to us that the whole of prophetic fulfillment cannot be relegated to the future, not when so much is happening now.

LITERALISM

At this point, we would likely be called upon to explain our-selves in terms of literal interpretations of prophecy, particu-larly those in the book of Revelation that may suggest a literal kingdom and a literal reign of one thousand years. For in read-ing our defense of the presence of the Holy Spirit within us and the kingdom of God among us, you would certainly not place us among the dispensationalists, whose literal view of the revelatory passages were advanced greatly during the last century, right through the *Left Behind* work of Tim LaHaye and Jerry Jenkins.

In many ways, we are literalists when it comes to Scripture. This makes unqualified sense in terms of narrative accounts and doctrinal passages like the epistles. But the Scriptures in-clude other forms of expression, such as poetry and prophecy, which often carry with them metaphors or even "veils" that limit our understanding if we lock them into one place, time, or perspective (consider the nature of Jesus' parables in this regard).

In truth, virtually no commentator, theologian, or pastor is an absolute literalist when it comes to Scripture. For instance, no one teaches that we should literally "cut off our right hand" if it causes us to sin, even though Jesus himself spoke these very words in the Sermon on the Mount.[65] No one argues—not now at least—that Jesus spoke literally of a typical human generation (roughly forty years) when he said, "I tell you the truth, this generation will certainly not pass away until all of these things have happened."[66]

For our frame of reference here, no one suggests that God

owns only "the cattle on a thousand hills."[67] And while some may argue that the meaning of "a thousand years is like a day, and a day is like a thousand years"[68] is literal in both aspects, these teachers are in the minority.

Therefore, when we begin to explore the prophecies of Revelation and we encounter references to 144,000 "sealed" representatives from the ancient Jewish tribes or the thousand-year reign of Christ, we do not automatically assume these to be literal numbers. We have already discussed (in chapter 7) what Paul could have meant when he wrote that "*all* Israel will be saved" in Romans 11—a vast majority but not *necessarily* all.

At the same time, there is an exactness in some of the language of Revelation—and even more so in the book of Daniel—that tempers our understanding. And we are awed with others who read the work of scholars who have uncovered apparent fulfillments or convergences that have fallen on meaningful specific days.[69]

WHO ARE THE TWO WITNESSES?

Perhaps the greatest question we would pose in the arena of literal versus non-literal interpretation considers the "two witnesses" of Revelation 11. Eschatologists have long tried to pin down the identity of these witnesses, who prophesy, work miracles, and take a martyr's stand against the beast that is unleashing evil on the planet. Normally, the resulting conclusion is that these are two men we have seen before in Scripture, perhaps Enoch and Elijah (who never died but were instead taken up into heaven) or Moses and Elijah (whose miracles resembled those enacted by the two witnesses in the Revelation 11 passage and who appeared with Jesus on the Mount of Transfiguration). Even those who do not suggest any two particular names point to the arrival of two men who will stand against the beast.

But there is a compellingly different possibility when we allow for a less literal interpretation of the two witnesses. Using both a symbolic hermeneutic and a general picture of the witnesses, Robert Mounce says this: "The two witnesses symbolize the entire worshiping community which bears collective witness to God and to God's Christ."[70]

As you might guess at this point, we would be more specific than Mounce, for we know that the "entire worshiping community" is made up of believing Jews and believing Gentiles. Could it be that the two witnesses of Revelation 11 are the believing Jew and the believing Gentile (in plurality), standing united in pronouncement and defense of our common Savior, who is Yeshua?

There is more to this than speculation based on our preference. Look closely at Revelation 11:4:

> **These are the two olive trees and the two lampstands that stand before the Lord of the earth.**

Now consider Zechariah 4:2:

> **He asked me, "What do you see?"**
> **I answered, "I see a solid gold lampstand with a bowl at the top and seven lights on it, with seven channels to the lights. Also there are two olive trees by it, one on the right of the bowl and the other on its left."**

Finally, be reminded of the language of Romans 11, which depicts Jews as "natural branches" of a cultivated olive tree and

Gentiles as "cut out of an olive tree that is wild by nature."

In the light of this recurring biblical reference to the paired olive trees, right into the midst of the picture of the two witnesses, we feel moved to ask whether it is possible that these two witnesses are——figuratively in light of the prophetic words but literally in light of their most certain existence on earth today——the believing Jews and the believing Gentiles who bear witness to the excellence and rulership of Christ?

THE SECOND COMING OF JESUS AND THE MILLENNIAL REIGN OF THE MESSIAH

Naturally, as we approach the end of our discussion about millennial matters, some readers must be wondering of us at this point, *If Jesus is already here, do you still believe that he is coming again?* To this we must quickly and unequivocally answer, Of course! While God occupies our hearts and our fellowship in him through the Holy Spirit (or Spirit of Christ), this does not mean that Jesus has ceased to exist as a member of the Trinity. He lives now at the right hand of the Father in heaven, but he will certainly return to reign on earth, according to Revelation, chapters 19 and 20. Both believing Jew and believing Gentile will thrill at the fulfillment of the Messiah coming triumphantly as the ever-reigning King of Kings and Lord of Lords, for he will come with undeniable identity as the victorious ruler sent from heaven (Revelation 19:11-16).

If, however, you are seeking from us a position as to when this will occur, while we would have to say that our current understanding causes us to lean toward a postmillennial picture, we would first have to defer to our earlier words about the lack of knowledge any of us possesses about a day or a time. Then we would have to acknowledge that our interest really lies in adding to the increasing exploration of a millennial po-

REPLACEMENT THEOLOGY

In its various forms, replacement theology "replaces" Israel with the church of Jesus Christ. All the unfulfilled biblical prophecies and promises originally intended for the Jewish people were given over to the church after Israel's rejection of Yeshua as Messiah. Historically, replacement theology has been linked to amillennial and postmillennial eschatology.

DUAL COVENANT THEOLOGY

Certain premillennial eschatologists could not agree with the transference to the church of the covenant promises made originally to Israel. But in their defense of Israel, these thinkers have allowed for a Jewish path to salvation differentiated from the Gentile path to salvation; only the latter must believe in Yeshua as the Messiah in order to be saved.

Toward a co-believing middle ground

A LARGE-SCALE JEWISH SPIRITUAL RESTORATION

An increasing number of theologians have grown uncomfortable with both of these positions and have called for an exploration of alternatives. We agree with this call, but humbly request that this exploration includes room for (a) a large-scale spiritual restoration of the Jewish people through Yeshua as Messiah, and (b) a Jewish return to the land of Israel.

sition that both honors the Jewish people and yet requires of them a profession of faith in Yeshua as Messiah.

The chart on the preceding page digs a little more deeply into this matter. An increasing number of theologians, both in Protestant and Catholic camps, are calling for a Jewish-inclusive eschatology that does not disqualify the Jewish people as "replacement theology" has done through the centuries.[71] As discussed in chapter 9, in this eschatological system, the prophecies and promises originally given to the people of Israel were "forfeited" by them when they rejected Yeshua as Messiah. These prophecies and promises have been passed on to the small believing remnant of Jews and the much larger number of Gentile believers, which together comprise the church. According to these theologians, there is no distinct future for the Jewish people. Our studies of Romans 9-11 (especially), along with similar studies by many others, do not allow us to accept this wholesale dismissal of the people who "are loved on account of the patriarchs."[72]

But these scholars, along with us, also struggle with the reaction to replacement theology, which is commonly called dual covenant theology. Under this structure, great latitude is given to the Jewish people—yea!—but few scriptural requirements are made of them either. Chief among these requirements would be the same thing required of all who would be saved by the Jewish Messiah: utter reliance on his righteousness over and above any that we could achieve through the Law. That is, those who would have their names written in the Lamb's Book of Life must identify with the Lamb, who is Yeshua Messiah, both in heart belief and tongue confession. Contrary to this requirement, dual covenant theologians allow for two paths to eternal relationship with God—a path for the Gentiles that requires such confessed faith in Jesus, but a path for the Jews that does not demand such a commitment. But in light of Scripture, we are no more able to accept this idea than we are able to accept replacement theology.

So there must be a new eschatological plan that threads its way between these two countering positions. It must, as we have already stated, simultaneously honor the Jewish people and Scripture's many specific promises to them and account for their necessary spiritual revival ("circumcision of the heart") through faith in Yeshua. Even if we were qualified to do so, we would not find room in a book like this one to lay out the intricacies of such a plan, including its impact on the major millennial systems that already exist. What we would do here, in keeping with all that we have discussed in this book, is humbly but earnestly ask that those who do endeavor to undertake such work do so with an eye to both the spiritual regeneration of the Jewish people *en masse* and to their claim to the land of Israel, as originally promised to Abraham and renewed through Moses by God. This request does nothing more than fall in line with our appreciation for the unveiling that is progressively occurring in our time, an unveiling that is revealing the turning of Jewish hearts as evidenced in the more than one hundred Messianic congregations and communities in an Israel wide open to those making *aliyah* today.

A GREATER DESIRE

When it comes to consideration of the end times, the truth is that most people declare themselves "pan-millennialists," explaining that they are sure that in God's hands "it will all pan out in the end." These people are not being flippant; they simply do not have the time to study the issues that theologians have, or their biblical interests lie in other arenas. Some even realize that the implications of a millennial position can be rather significant when leading to other practices, such as evangelism or social action. In this case, there are those who still avoid millennial discussions simply because they are uncomfortable with the contention that can arise from the discussion surrounding the various positions.

Others, however, are more than comfortable, at least with the studying required to become knowledgeable in the arguments for and against each position. They study the Scriptures, read the theologies, and emerge with a rather firm position in one camp or another, each one "convinced in his own mind." Certainly, there is no shame in this, as long as we continue as the body of Christ to emphasize above all things him who is our head, Jesus.

Therefore, we have left our own eschatological leanings somewhat uncovered. Because our chief desire is to see Jews and Gentiles, men and women and children turn to Jesus, we have spent far more time in this book on those matters. Because on this we can all agree: those who believe in their heart and confess with their mouth that Jesus is Lord will be saved. No matter what course or timeline God takes in closing the old earth and old heaven and replacing them with the new earth and new heaven, our common desire as followers of Jesus is to multiply ourselves—that is, to invite more and more people into the kingdom of God, through our words and through the actions that authenticate those words. We cannot do this if we are in the habit of discounting people because of their ethnicities, traditions or currently held philosophies, be they Jews, Muslims, Buddhists, nominal Christians, atheists, or whatever else. If we and you need Jesus, so do they. In this regard, sooner is always better than later.

THE CHAPTER IN REVIEW

End Times Implications

ONE BIG IDEA

The discussion of prophecy invites various questions about end times occurrences. Though some set out to provide clear cut answers to these matters, a better approach may be to open more questions.

KEY POINTS

• *Jesus affirmed that the time of his return is unknowable to anyone on earth.*

• *A complete end times theology should include both the return of the Jewish people to the land of Israel and a return of their hearts to God.*

• *Although some people are looking for a rebuilding of the temple in Jerusalem, we are keen to the New Testament presentation of our own selves as "temples of the Lord." In fact, several aspects often relegated to future fulfillment are already in place.*

• *Strict literalism in reviewing prophetic passages presents several problems.*

• *The two witnesses of Revelation may well be believing Jews and believing Gentiles united in testimony.*

• *Jesus is coming again!*

CLOSING WORDS
FLATTENING THE MOUNTAINS

IT IS ONE OF THE MOST INTRIGUING LINES IN ALL of Scripture. Recorded in two separate instances, Jesus told his disciples that if they had faith the size of a mustard seed, they could move mountains. Really, Jesus? Mountains? It's just so hard to imagine the possibility.

Before we close this book, we want to explore with you what Jesus could possibly have meant when he spoke these words, first below the mountain on which he was transfigured, then later outside Jerusalem. We think you will be amazed to find that Jesus really is calling us to such a work in his kingdom as we prepare for "the end of the age."

In the 41st chapter of Isaiah, God spoke through the prophet concerning the scattered, discouraged state of the Jewish people. Then God offered this:

"All who rage against you
    will surely be ashamed and disgraced;
those who oppose you
    will be as nothing and perish.
Though you search for your enemies,
    you will not find them.

> Those who wage war against you
> will be as nothing at all.
> For I am the LORD, your God,
> who takes hold of your right hand
> and says to you, Do not fear;
> I will help you.
> Do not be afraid, O worm, Jacob,
> O little Israel,
> for I myself will help you," declares the LORD,
> your Redeemer, the Holy One of Israel.
> "See, I will make you into a threshing sledge,
> new and sharp, with many teeth.
> You will thresh the mountains and crush them,
> and reduce the hills to chaff.
> You will winnow them, the wind will pick them up,
> and a gale will blow them away.
> But you will rejoice in the LORD
> and glory in the Holy One of Israel."
> (Isaiah 41:11-16)

We see two fascinating things in this passage. First, we see the protective love of God for the people of Israel. Though they are small ("O little Israel") and disregarded ("O worm, Jacob"), God is on their side. But we also see God's plan for this people, that they will become mountain crushers.

What could this possibly mean? We suggest that God meant here—and Jesus meant when he spoke to his disciples of moving mountains—that there are obstacles that will come between us and God. These are obstacles that will be moved by the people of God, believing Jews and believing Gentiles, for the sake of the salvation of the world.

Consider the context of the passages where Jesus spoke of faith's power to move mountains. The first came at the healing of a demon-possessed boy, who was being convulsed and thrown into fire and water by the demon within him. Jesus rebuked the demon, and the boy was healed. When the disciples asked why they could not drive out this demon themselves, as they had done with other demons, Jesus replied, "Because you have so little faith. I tell you the truth, if you have faith as small as a mustard seed, you can say to this mountain, 'Move from here to there' and it will move. Nothing will be impossible for you."[73]

One clear obstacle that stands between sinful man and the holy, saving God is the direct influence of the enemy, Satan. Paul's words are still true: "Our battle is not against flesh and blood...but against the powers of this dark world."[74] Those who have faith in Jesus will be able to thresh this mountain—not in their own strength, for there is grave danger in that, but by the power of the Holy Spirit living in them.

The second instance of Jesus' pronouncement that those of faith would move mountains is recorded both in Matthew 21 and Mark 11. The Matthew passage presents the scenario a bit more succinctly; here it is:

Early in the morning, as he was on his way back to the city, he was hungry. Seeing a fig tree by the road, he went up to it but found nothing on it except leaves. Then he said to it, "May you never bear fruit again!" Immediately the tree withered.

When the disciples saw this, they were amazed. "How did this fig tree wither so quickly?" they asked.

> Jesus replied, "I tell you the truth, if you have
> faith and do not doubt, not only can you do what
> was done to the fig tree, but also you can say to
> this mountain, 'Go, throw yourself into the sea,'
> and it will be done." (Matthew 21:18-21)

On the surface, this seems like a gratuitous, even nasty, miracle. Certainly, Jesus was not against fig trees! But we know without a doubt that he was against fruitless religion. Whenever he encountered it, he confronted and rebuked it. Too often in the history of Israel, the people turned from fruitful faith in God to religiosity and idol worship. The prophet Hosea recorded these words of God:

> "When I found Israel,
>   it was like finding grapes in the desert;
> when I saw your fathers,
>   it was like seeing the early fruit on the fig tree.
> But when they came to Baal Peor,
>   they consecrated themselves to that shameful
>   idol
>   and became as vile as the thing they loved."
> (Hosea 9:10)

God saw the potential of delicious fruit from the "fig tree" that was Israel. Then he saw that potential exchanged for worthless religion pointed at a lifeless idol. Jesus' cursing of the fig tree was indicative of these same words of the Father, that such fruitlessness was "vile."

Again, those of faith can serve Yeshua as people enabled to bring down the mountains of fruitlessness that present obstacles for those who would know the Savior. This is not a violent work, or one done by mustering up one's own courage or strength. This is the work of the Elisha ministry, rendered only by the Holy Spirit's guidance and power. It may be done by Jews or Gentiles, but it must be done by people of faith in Jesus, and it is best done when the body of believers is functioning in its full unity and diversity. It does not reflect a Jewish mindset or a Gentile mindset. It does not reflect Western culture or Eastern culture. It does not reflect Israeli or Arab or Asian or European or American. It does not reflect one denomination or another. It reflects Jesus as Messiah, our only hope.

And so we end where we began. This is a book of hope. It calls upon the Spirit of God to rise up among his people. This must come first. Then it urges the people to rise to that call, living and loving as Christ's holy ones.

In truth, we see this already happening. Believing Jews in Israel are welcoming their Semitic brothers and sisters, encouraging them too to call upon the Name Above All Names—that's right, Jews are loving Arabs. Orthodox Jews would do no such thing; their separatism under the guise of religion does not allow for it. Secular Jews would do no such thing; they have no lasting hope to offer. Only those Jews who are in Jesus dare "go and do likewise," being the true neighbor to those who are dying without Yeshua, no matter how dangerous the personal sacrifices may be.

The two of us writing this book, and many who are reading it, are Gentiles. For too long, we have in overt and subtle ways considered our faith superior to that of the Jewish people. But if we dare to look at Romans 11:30-32 honestly, we know that the difficulties of the Jews—even if they appear to be of their own faithless making—have come about for our sake. God has permitted the disobedience of the Jews to draw us to him.

How odd is the sovereignty of our Lord! But it is *his* sovereignty, and we are called to live under it. Thus, we must find a heart of mercy like his own, a heart now given back to the Jewish people that they too may gain the mercy of God. We may feel wholly unequipped to do this work. After all, we are not Jewish. That is exactly why we must begin with the infilling of the Holy Spirit. Apart from him, we can do nothing! And it is why we cannot come to the work alone, but must come together with our believing Jewish friends. They know the God of Abraham, Isaac, and Jacob—and they know his beloved Son. United with them, we go not only with the blessing of Elijah, but with the double blessing of Elisha. We go in the name of Yahweh, in the nature of Yeshua, in the power of the Holy Spirit, and in the spirit of love. This is not just hope—it is our *only* hope if we truly desire to land in the flow of what God plans for the culminating age and the establishment of his eternal kingdom.

APPENDIX
A LETTER TO MY JEWISH FRIENDS

DEAR FELLOW WORSHIPER OF THE GOD OF ABRA-
HAM, ISAAC AND JACOB,

I have no reason to believe that this book has been read by many who would consider themselves traditional Jews of the Orthodox or Reform camps. However, I have been so frequently surprised in my life to find myself in conversation with a Jewish man or woman, that I know there are some of you who have committed the time and the thought to read the words we have set down here.

Through the years, I have had the incredible opportunity to share my walk with Jesus with many precious Jewish friends. There is the obvious discomfort of having them feel as though I am trying to coax them away from their Jewish heritage and into my Gentile religion. This is frustrating! It is, of course, the natural by-product of hundreds of years of anti-Semitism within the church, as well as the traditional teaching from many rabbis that once a person "converts" to Christianity they are no longer Jewish. It's time to address this issue head-on. Knowing such history, an emotional response is entirely acceptable. But we cannot forget also to engage our minds in the logical consideration of Judaism and Yeshua.

First, for individual Jewish people to embrace a Jewish Messiah because they honestly believe that he was the fulfillment of both the Law and the Prophets should be both natural and expected. If, after a thorough examination of all the prophets had foreseen, they still don't believe that Jesus fulfilled the needed requirements, they should walk the other way. Yeshua (Jesus) himself made such a bold claim when he stated, "Do not believe me unless I do what my Father does. But if I do it, even though you do not believe me, believe the miracles, that you may know and understand that the Father is in me, and I in the Father" (John 10:37-38). This was the presentation that Saul of Tarsus (the apostle Paul) made in every synagogue he entered. Some believed and some did not.

This was the simple beginning of the church——Jews shared the good news with other Jews. Some believed and some did not. This should strike us as normal. The prophets experienced the same mixture of both acceptance and rejection. Isaiah, Jeremiah, Ezekiel, and others all had their "disciples" (see Isaiah 8:16) and their impassioned detractors. But this is where it gets strange. Why would Gentiles, who loved the idea of worshipping gods they had created for their own benefit, be interested in a God wholly introduced to them by Jews——a God who talked of eternal accountability and judgment?

You see, my frustration rests with this thought: I have been introduced to a Jewish God through a Jewish Messiah, and it has changed my life. I had absolutely nothing prior to that! As Paul plainly stated in reference to Gentiles like me, I was "...excluded from citizenship in Israel, and [a foreigner] to the covenants of promise, without hope and without God in the world" (Ephesians 2:12). How has this miraculous happening been mysteriously changed into a Gentile religion? It is not a Gentile religion, and it never was.

Regardless of the Nicene Creed, the imposition of "Christian" holidays masking the reality of the Jewish festivals, and an uneducated and underinformed church after Constantine, the fact is that God revealed himself to and through the Jews. I was introduced to the God of Abraham, Isaac and Jacob through the Jewish conduit. How is this possible? Only by the Jewish Messiah, who came first to the Jewish people, but ultimately to the entire world. As Yeshua so plainly stated, "God did not send his Son into the world to condemn the world, but to save the world through him" (John 3:17).

It is not strange that a Jew would believe in a Jewish Messiah. But it is very strange that a Gentile like me would ditch everything, realize that he has nothing, and reach out for what more and more Jews realize to be true today: the Jewish Savior, who is Yeshua of Nazareth, changes lives!

In some Christian traditions, it is typical after a statement like this to offer an "invitation" to come to Jesus. No such invitation needs to be given to the Jewish man or woman, for their own Scriptures have been calling out to them for hundreds of years: "'Even now,' declares the LORD, 'return to me with all your heart'" (Joel 2:12). For you, the call is different. It is to come to God who has come to us as Immanuel. He came to walk among his own people, to offer his own life, to provide the only way to his eternal presence through the perfect and lasting sacrifice. This is what I invite you to consider. This is what I invite you to take hold of for yourself.

Most sincerely,
Jeffrey Cranford
Fall 2010

NOTES

1 Because of differences in how certain individual prophecies may be interpreted, it is not possible to offer an exact numeric comparison here. However, all lists we could produce would demonstrate the preeminence of the spiritual regeneration prophecies. Many will be mentioned throughout this book.

2 Some special notes should be made here with regard to biblical sacrifice, for those who are unfamiliar with this may be taken aback at the mention of this ritual. (a) The sacrifices were made by priests, who were responsible for ensuring that the act was done according to Mosaic instruction. (b) Animals without blemish were called for in biblical sacrifice, and most were bred for this special purpose. (c) Unless the law called for a complete destruction of the animal by incineration, after the animal was killed and its blood drained, it was set aside for consumption by priests, who were neither farmers nor herders. (d) In the Mosaic law, the sacrifice of humans was strictly forbidden and punishable by death.

3 Read John 4:23-24: "'Yet a time is coming and has now come when the true worshipers will worship the Father in spirit and in truth, for they are the kind of worshipers the Father seeks. God is spirit and his worshipers must worship him in spirit and in truth.'"

4 1 Corinthians 1:23

5 Galatians 3:28

6 As recently as early 2009, Messianic Jews were expressing to reporter Michele Chabin of Religion News Service that they were experiencing "an unprecedented level of harassment." This has included protests, burning of buildings and automobiles, revocation of business certification, and the bombing of homes. http://www.crosswalk.com/news/religiontoday/11624326/

7 The words of Jesus himself in no way allow for such a singular claim against the Jews. Read Luke 18:31-33: "Jesus took the Twelve aside and told them, 'We are going up to Jerusalem, and everything that is written by the prophets about the Son of Man [Jesus] will be fulfilled. He will be handed over to the Gentiles. They will mock him, insult him, spit on him, flog him and kill him. On the third day, he will rise again.'" That is, the Jewish leaders handed a Jewish man over to the Gentiles, who then, in camaraderie with the Jews, put Jesus to death. The responsibility for the death of Jesus Christ rests *jointly* with Jews and Gentiles.

8 Ephesians 6:12

9 Osama bin Laden and Iranian president Mahmoud Ahmadinejad are among those who have announced such deadly intentions for the Jewish people in Israel and abroad (chiefly in the United States and Europe) and who have made efforts to gather and build weapons for such attacks. Those who are interested in these matters particularly would do best to read the works of Joel Rosenberg.

10 Isaiah 66:22. A similar promise is found in Jeremiah 31:35-36.

11 Some readers at this stage may be concerned that we are taking a position of "sympathy" for Israel, akin to a particular political stance of support. At a later stage, we will offer some insight into the contemporary nation of Israel and its apparent role in God's unfolding plan for the ages, but a political sort of sympathy is not what we are speaking of in this particular context. Rather, we are saying that as believers in Jesus Christ, we follow in the God-ordained lineage that began with Abraham, continued through his physical descendants, and has worked its way into our own hearts because of Jesus. For this reason, we should have a familial place in our hearts for the Jewish people; thus, we should not hesitate to express grief and remorse for the persecution that has harmed the Jewish people throughout history, especially when we know that some of that persecution was delivered by the hands of those who claimed to bear the name of Christ.

12 You may appreciate a simple but ambitious list at http://bibleprobe.com/365messianicprophecies.htm, while we also consider quite helpful the supporting explanations offered at http://www.clarifyingchristianity.com/m_prophecies.shtml.

13 Ephesians 2:14-16

14 Luke 7:9

15 Matthew 15:27

16 Verses quoted: Acts 10:45 and 11:18

17 John 12:23-24

18 For further understanding about the principle of the stumbling stone, see Psalm 118:22 and Isaiah 8:14.

19 Galatians 3:28

20 Ephesians 2:15. We completely understand at this stage that if you are a non-believing Jew who has rejected Jesus as the promised Messiah this suggestion of "one new man" may be quite offensive to you. We would simply ask that you place this statement not on our lips but on the lips of Paul, the Jewish Pharisee of Jesus' own time, who was moved by the Holy Spirit of God from a life of persecuting Christ-followers (even giving consent and direction for their deaths) to a belief in Jesus so strong it led him to personal sacrifice and his own death for his faith in and ministry in the name of Jesus. Paul never surrendered his Jewish heritage, only the bounds of prideful self-righteousness that it laid on him as a Pharisee, trading them for what he often called freedom in Christ.

21 We can find similar passages about the progressive unveiling that occurred with Jesus' first coming and the salvation he brought in Hebrews 1:1-2 and 1 Peter 1:10-12.

22 Again, we use the expression "non-believing Jews" to encompass those who would classify themselves as Orthodox Jews, adhering strictly to the laws of the Torah on a daily basis, as well as to those who would consider themselves less strict but certainly committed to the traditional flow of Judaism and most of its legal-religious aspects. No matter the disagreements they may have between themselves about who is "truly Jewish," all non-believing Jews would insist that Yeshua of Nazareth was not the promised Messiah and that Messiah is yet to come.

23 Interestingly, the Wikipedia entry for *aliyah* does a tidy job of outlining the numerous organized returns of Jewish people to the land of Israel (pre-1948) and to the land and nation of Israel (post-1948), with links to further discussions about each of these separate immigrations (eighteen in all).

24 We have purposefully here elected to use the expression "God's voice" as opposed to the original "decrees and laws" in deference to Paul's teaching to the Galatians 3:19 — "What, then, was the purpose of the law? It was added because of transgressions until the Seed to whom the promise referred (Jesus) had come." This absolutely includes an obedience to God himself, perhaps even advocating certain essentials (such as the four items set forth in the Jerusalem Council of Acts 15). But because there will be some degree of variation between Jews and Gentiles and their various congregations as to the decrees and laws that are certainly applicable today, we have chosen to express the directions of God as "God's voice" for both (a) believers universally and (b) believers in local settings.

25 1 Peter 4:17

26 Dual fulfillment is a commonly accepted theological explanation for prophecies that have been fulfilled at one point in history but which also appear to have future meaning. Some theologians would suggest that certain prophecies stretch beyond a dual fulfillment, with multiple fulfillments taking place through history and possibly into the future.

27 Isaiah 49:6

28 Amos 3:7

29 Other prophetic passages where we see this kind of Spirit-led revival are: Isaiah 32:14-20, Isaiah 44:1-5, and Ezekiel 36:24-28.

30 Other prophetic passages where we see this kind of humble regret and repentance before God are Zechariah 12:10-14, and Jeremiah 50:4-5. And one to exhort this kind of godly grief: James 4:9-10.

31 We are indebted in our thinking to the confirming work of John Piper, particularly in his sermon, "All Israel Will Be Saved," of February 29, 2004, available online at http://www.desiringgod.org/ResourceLibrary/Sermons/ByScripture/10/164_All_Israel_Will_Be_Saved. While Piper has sometimes been dismissed as unsympathetic to the Jewish cause, this sermon certainly suggests otherwise.

32 http://www.israelnationalnews.com/News/News.aspx/138149

33 Matthew 24:12

34 Genesis 12:3

35 1 Thessalonians 3:8

36 Revelation 21:4

37 We fully understand that many Jewish people, and particularly Orthodox Jews, consider the suggestion that Jewish people must come to belief in Yeshua as Messiah a form of anti-Semitism. There is virtually no way around this difficulty, other than to continue expressing the love of Christ to the greatest degree possible and relying on the softening work of the Holy Spirit in the hearts of those who would come to belief.

38 Romans 11:29

39 Isaiah 60:10 records "Foreigners will rebuild your walls, and their kings will serve you," while Isaiah 61:5 says, "Aliens will shepherd your flocks; foreigners will work your fields and vineyards." In both the physical and spiritual applications of these prophecies, there is opportunity to be one who sows among the Jews a restorative seed unto God's ultimate work in them.

40 See Isaiah 45:11-13, and also Isaiah 44:28. Both 2 Chronicles 36:22 and Ezra 1:1 also identify Cyrus' work as a fulfillment of Jeremiah's prophecies, though the exact passage to those prophecies is unknown.

41 Ezra 1:2

42 There are several parallels between the lives and ministries of Elijah and John the Baptist: (1) Both were provided for in the wilderness prior to the emergence of their ministries; (2) both were strongly opposed by the wives of wicked kings; (3) both leaned toward a message of "justice in time" rather than of mercy; and (4) both experienced questions of faith in the midst of personal crisis.

43 While the count varies depending on the detail of the expositor, agreement remains that the count is two to one in favor of Elisha. David Pyles lists 14 miracles under Elijah's ministry and 28 under Elisha's at http://www.bcbsr.com/survey/eli.html. Meanwhile, Michael Hunt counts eight for Elijah and 16 for Elisha at http://www.agapebiblestudy.com/charts/Miracles%20of%20Elijah%20and%20Elisha.htm. Still others come up with a difference of 14 to seven.

44 We want to be certain to add into this context our awareness that many believers now are increasingly aware of the need of people throughout the world for fresh water. While developed countries have drawn good water from the ground through advanced wells for decades, those in the savannas of Africa and the overrun cities of Asia and South America have not had this same sort of access. They must journey long distances to draw water from clean water sources, or risk drinking contaminated water—a risk that invariably leads to disease and death. Among both secular and the "faith-based" populations, organizations helping address this problem in affordable and life-giving ways have arisen in increasing numbers in recent years. This is a literal application of the "fresh water" kingdom work that is to be done in our world, a work that we believe should be representative of the love of God through his people. Indeed, while countries that have closed the doors to Jesus (sometimes violently) have fallen into structural disrepair, a stark contrast can be presented by those who represent Jesus and offer the most meaningful of infrastructure aids, fresh water. (Well-known Middle East observer and writer Joel Rosenberg has reported the deteriorating conditions in countries like Afghanistan and Iran in his book, *Inside the Revolution: How the Followers of Jihad, Jefferson, & Jesus Are Battling to Dominate the Middle East and Transform the World*. Afghanistan and Iran, particularly, are two countries that have in recent years fought openly against Christian influence in their countries and Jewish presence in the region. The typical structure in non-democratic Middle Eastern and African countries allows for an extremely wealthy minority elite attached to the oil trade and/or political power, an empowered military to support these leaders, and a severely impoverished—and sometimes persecuted—remainder class, the latter of which has severely limited or no access to what we would consider "basic services.")

45 2 Kings 3:15-17

46 An inquiry at YouTube regarding Jewish-Arab worship reveals several excellent examples of this phenomenon. We recommend starting here: http://www.youtube.com/watch?v=XK6NtWYwbZM

47 2 Kings 5:15

48 John 4:20

49 Ephesians 5:25-26

50 See Jeremiah 5:10-11, Ezekiel 19:11-14, and Romans 11:17-21. Of course, we would also do well to be aware of the imagery of the abiding branches spoken of by Jesus in John 15:1-8.

51 2 Corinthians 4:17-18

52 We are told in 2 Kings 7:6 that the reason for this abandonment was that the LORD had caused the Arameans to hear a sound like chariots and horses. They assumed that the Israelites had engaged some powerful allies, and the Arameans fled for their lives.

53 Matthew 23:23

54 One of our favorite sites in Israel today is Yad Hashmona, a *moshav* (community and retreat center) built with funding by the Finnish government in self-imposed restitution for their surrender of eight Jewish refugees to the Nazis during World War II. While the Finnish government is not a "believing church," they worked with the church in Finland beginning in 1971 to provide richly for this center in the hills of Israel. Here are the resources of the Gentiles being given for the sake of the Jews. More wonderfully, from our perspective, the community of about 150 residents at Yad Hashmona is comprised of "living stones," Jewish men and women who have a completed Jewish faith in Yeshua as Messiah.

55 Revelation 3:15-16. Of course, God conveys here that he prefers "hot or cold" to lukewarm. But his certain preference would be for us to be "hot" for him—that is, fully committed to him, rather than marginally so.

56 Acts 26:22-23

57 Psalm 122:8

58 2 Kings 5:27. We know that throughout Scripture, the Hebrew and Greek words normally translated "leprosy" carry an ambiguous meaning, which may have pointed to actual disabling and (at the time) highly contagious leprosy, or to many other kinds of discoloring or disfiguring skin diseases.

59 James 4:10; Isaiah 66:2; John 4:23-24

60 Saucy's work is the oldest here; it is *The Case for Progressive Dispensationalism* (Zondervan, 1993), followed in 2000 by Blasing and Bock's *Progressive Dispensationalism* (Baker Academic). While progressive dispensationalism adamantly holds to the continuing prophetic promises that will be delivered to believing Israel separate from believing Gentiles, there are other aspects of the system that we would not adhere to from our own understanding of Scriptures. Chan's work is an unpublished paper titled "Exploring a Fourth Millennial Position: On the Applicability of Israel's Old Testament National Restoration Promises to the Growing Messianic Jewish Movement." Its questions and suggestions were among the seeds for the book you are now reading. In the spirit of what we are saying here, Chan completed his paper with this paragraph: "We have essentially set forth a new paradigm by which to read OT prophetic texts. The success or failure of any new conceptual construct, of course, depends upon how well it explains all the necessary data. It still needs to be seen whether Jewish restoration postmillennialism can offer convincing interpretations to the great 'millennial' texts of the Bible. Even if it does not, we are certain the process of dialogue will sharpen arguments for the other views and generate whole new areas of inquiry."

61 Acts 17:24

62 Drawn by Paul from Leviticus 26:12, Jeremiah 32:38, and Ezekiel 37:27.

63 Drawn by Paul from Isaiah 52:11 and Ezekiel 20:34, 41.

64 Some commentators contribute this quoted passage to 2 Samuel 7:14 and even 2 Samuel 7:8.

65 Matthew 5:29-30

66 Luke 21:32

67 Psalm 20:10

68 2 Peter 3:8

69 Perhaps our favorite among such work is that of Rick Larson in researching the Star of Bethlehem (www.bethlehemstar.net). This work offers overwhelming evidence that God does work with stunning precision, even in reference to days and times, though this work is normally recognized by us only in hindsight.

70 Mounce, Robert. *The Book of Revelation (The New International Commentary on the New Testament)*, (Grand Rapids, Mich.: Eerdmans, 1997).

71 As a sampling of such scholarship, we would point to

Ronald Diprose and Barry E. Horner, as well as the Jewish Catholic theologian Roy Schoeman.

72 Romans 11:28

73 Matthew 17:20

74 Ephesians 6:12

Breinigsville, PA USA
12 December 2010
251236BV00003B/2/P